Voices

from the

Middle

Voices from the Middle

A memoir

Michele M. Chamberlain

This book is a memoir of real events
.

Student contributions used with permission. In some cases, names or specific details have been altered to protect the identity of individuals mentioned herein.

For more information, contact the author at
VoicesfromtheMiddle2019@gmail.com

Cover Art by Katherine Heins

ISBN: 9781696469586

Dedicated to all my Chamberlain kids.

You know who you are.

Acknowledgements

There are many people who came together to ensure the publication of this memoir. You have my profound thanks and gratitude.

First and foremost, to my editor, Jo Sahlin, for your dedication to this project and belief in the importance of its message.

To my pre-readers: Rachel Pack, Melanie McGuire, Kam Morrill, Amelia Day, Jennifer Eide and Ira Allen. Your initial feedback on the rough draft was invaluable to this process. Thank you for volunteering so enthusiastically to be part of this journey.

To my friend and colleague, Ira Allen. Your contributions both in my classroom and on this manuscript were without equal. Your excitement about this project propelled me forward. Thank you for your many hours of collaboration as a reader, editor and classroom co-conspirator.

To my students who contributed their voices to this story in the chapter introductions: Natalie, Amelia, Cooper, Mattias, Cali, Ethan, Aden, Kiara, Michael, Kaitlyn, and Mason. Your powerful words and perspectives were essential to the telling of these stories.

To the many, many Chamberlain kids mentioned in these pages: thank you allowing me to share your joys and challenges from our time together in 8th grade science. I am a better person for knowing each of you and for the lessons you've taught me.

To Izzie, Micah, Jetmir and Kayla. You are in my heart.

A special thanks to the many parents who enthusiastically supported the participation and meaningful contributions of your sons and daughters.

To my colleagues Patty, Doug, Gino, Eric, Brian, Jim, Dan and Heather: thank you for your friendship. The memories of our experiences in busy classrooms and shared hallways helped shape the development of this story.

To my daughters Katie and Emma: you were my initial inspiration for becoming a teacher many years ago. Without your support and love, none of this would have happened.

For my husband, Ted. You believed in this story, and my ability to tell it, long before I did. I love you.

Foreward

While I would never claim to be an expert on the public education system in the U.S., I am a product of that system and have been volunteering in public school classrooms for the last five years. As a physician, I know the value of education and the credibility it confers upon the well-educated. Yes, education opens doors and provides opportunities. But for some students, educational success is difficult within the context of the cookie-cutter, one-size-fits-all paradigm that is our public school system. True learning, a process that prepares children for a fulfilling adult life, requires a more holistic approach—one that recognizes not only a child's individual strengths and weaknesses, but their unique cultural and socioeconomic circumstances.

Amazing teachers—I call them rockstar teachers—like Michele do not simply follow a prescribed set of educational standards but find a way to make a meaningful connection with each of their students. Their superpowers are manifest in their ability to forge real relationships with their students, where mutual trust, respect, and friendship set the foundation for learning. I know this about Michele because I was in the trenches with her every Tuesday for three years, watching her work her brand of superhero magic in each of her classes.

As a classroom volunteer, I have been carefully observing, and learning from, several teachers in two school districts. They all strive, with unbelievable dedication and determination, to find ways to make a difference in the lives of their students. The education system sometimes supports them; at other times it is not their friend, but more like an anchor that holds them back—like trying to swim while wearing ankle weights. To be fair, it is often not the system that fails our teachers—and, consequently, some of our children—but the lack of resources to effectively provide an optimal learning experience tailored for every child's unique circumstances.

Michele tells the raw truth about what it is like to be an 8th grade science teacher. Warts and scars are uncovered for all to see. She brings us face to face with the realities of our public education system, compelling us to stand up and say—no, scream: "We can do better for our children!"

If you are a teacher or want to become one—particularly a middle school teacher—this book is a must-read.

If you are a parent, or plan to become one, you owe it to your children to read this book.

If you are retired like I am, you have skills and life experience...and time. Get your ass into a classroom and help a teacher! Our children are the future, and they deserve the very best education we can provide. Even the dedication and hard work of the finest rockstar teachers will never be enough to reach every student in our resource-deprived public-school system. Your help can make a difference.

Go find your starfish!

Ira S. Allen, MD

Retired Pathologist and Clinical Laboratory Medical Director,

Bellevue, WA

The Routine

It's Saturday morning and I am awake early.

I always wake up early. The shades in my bedroom are closed as tightly as they will go to protect against the late-August sunrise, but I am in no danger of being woken by the sun.

I can hear my husband's voice in my brain, chiding me. "Don't exaggerate," it says. "Sometimes you do sleep until 6."

Okay. Not always. Almost always.

I roll over and grab my phone to check the time.

5:09 a.m.

Ohhhhhhh... fuck.

I know there is no point in trying to roll over for a few more minutes of sleep. My body is so used to getting up early during the week I am unable to sleep-in any other time– weekends, holidays, summers. It is the curse of being a teacher.

The blue light from my phone screen is glaring and harsh, so I turn it off. Quietly, I make my way out of the bedroom into a space where I hopefully won't disturb the rest of the household. Our three dogs demand to follow me to my quiet space, and as we walk, they jockey for position to get as close to me as possible without touching each other. This is a game we play on the weekends. There is a certain amount of vying for space as they wait for me to settle with my computer and a cup of hot coffee. Stella ends up on the couch snuggled next to me. Ernie sits on the back of the couch where he can see my screen. I reach up behind me and give him a quick pat. He is my little buddy. Amy, our greyhound, doesn't compete for any coveted couch space; instead, she takes up residence in her comfy bed on the floor right next to the couch. Everyone is in position. We are ready for our weekend morning ritual of answering emails, reviewing publications, and reading science news that contains headlines like, "New protoplanet discovered 40 light years from Earth" or, "Plastic eating microbes could be the answer to ocean pollution." During the school year, if I am feeling super energetic, I might even venture into a student's online Google Drive and browse through their science folders for a reflection to read or to add encouragement to a student who is struggling through an assignment or research paper. I amuse myself by pondering what a parent must think when they receive an email response or a course syllabus from me time stamped at 5:32 a.m. There is a little temptation to pat myself on the back for being so dedicated and organized. The truth is, though, I am a creature of habit, and my zealous work ethic has more to do with routine than any superpowers.

The only disturbance to the quiet is the sharp staccato of my fingernails tapping on the keyboard, and I am acutely aware of breaking this silence. Only my right hand has fingernails long enough to hit against the keys; on my left hand, I keep the nails short for playing guitar. The result is a broken rhythm: two clicks, an awkward space where my fingers hit the "e" and "s" keys, and then more clicks. The dogs don't seem to mind the discordant sounds. They are used to them by now.

We work uninterrupted until the rest of the household begins to stir and it's time to tuck my work away for a few hours. Walking away from my computer is easy, but the upcoming week nags at me the rest of the day.

--------- ------- -------

Sunday evenings are just as eventful as Saturday mornings. My job at the end of the weekend is to make sure I am ready for the mayhem of the week that awaits. On my list of duties is always the obligatory run to the grocery store to grab a few last-minute supplies and make sure I have enough snacks (or" snackage"–a term my students coined a few years ago) to make it through an entire week of 8th grade.

Early on in my teaching career I wasn't quite so liberal in my use of food in the classroom. It would probably be fair to say I was a bit of a hard ass on this issue. ("This is a science classroom! We can't have food in here!"). I am sure former students who are reading this book will be sad to discover this fact. Despite breakfast and lunch programs offered in school, students still showed up to my classes hungry. For some, particularly students living in an emotional or economic crisis, school was their only consistent source of nutrition. One day I was in front of the class enthusiastically teaching about the difference between kinetic and potential energy and doing my very best to be clear, yet lively and engaging. I noticed a student had his head down on his desk, and I chided him a bit for not paying attention. He looked right at me and said, "I'm sorry, Mrs. C. I'm hungry."

I still feel ashamed, remembering his unwavering voice and seeing the despair in his eyes. I gave him an apple and granola bar from my own lunch. After that, I decided I would keep an arsenal of granola bars and fruit snacks in class. This moment was a philosophical turning point for me; hungry students cannot learn. Why did it take me so long to learn this lesson?

Food is the universal language of hope.

And hope can be hard to find… and easy to lose.

By the time students reach 8th grade, they have spent years learning about their academic strengths and weaknesses. Students have already decided before they set foot in my door whether they are good at science, and they have no problem telling me (to my face) how much they hate my class, or even how much they hate me.

Why?

Because at 13 years old, they have learned through repeated failure they cannot ever be successful in a science class. They have already lost hope. Every year I watch those reluctant, disengaged learners evolve into curious students who discover–perhaps for the first time–the joy of success. If I can help them along this path with a granola bar or Fruit Roll-Up, it is a small price to pay.

Evenings at the grocery store are surprisingly busy. A better time to come would be early mornings, but of course, that would interfere with my stalwart weekend morning routine, so I am stuck with the evening crowd. The hustle and bustle of the grocery store doesn't bother me, and I don't mind waiting in line. The part of this trip with which I actually struggle is what happens when it is finally my turn to unload my cart.

I try to put the more mundane items out first: a loaf of bread, some bananas, a quart of milk, some yogurt. Then comes the snackage. Jolly Ranchers always are common, as are plain granola bars, Goldfish crackers (or crackers of any kind, really– my kids love crackers). Organic fruit snacks make the list. And invariably, there will be a box of donuts–or several boxes, depending on the intensity of the week ahead. I finish unloading my groceries: two boxes of lovely Ticonderoga pencils, an extra composition notebook, and a pack of sticky notes. And I wait for the inevitable conversation that will go something like this:

"Hey there, hon! Welcome to Safeway. D'ya have your rewards card?"

"Uhm… I can't find my card." I can never find my card. It is probably buried under a pile of snackage in my classroom. "Can I give you the phone number instead?"

"Oh sure, no problem. Just use the keypad to enter it. How's yer day been, hon?"

"Oh good, you know. Just busy. Getting a lot of work done."

"Oh yep, yep," she replies as she quickly scans through my distractor groceries. Now I see her grab the economy sized bag of Jolly Ranchers. She slides it expertly across the scanner and back into my now-empty cart.

"It looks like yer having a party, here, hon?"

I cringe a little. "Uhm… well, I am a teacher. I'm just getting my supplies ready for the week."

"Oh, yer a teacher. Oh, that's GREAT!" She draws this word out a little bit, so it sounds more like graaaayte. "My uncle Martin's wife, Susan, is a teacher." Her enthusiasm bubbles over. "I just LOVE teachers. Why y'all just work so HARD. I see teachers coming in all the time to buy things for their classrooms. What grade d'ya teach, hon?"

And here it comes…

"Well, I teach 8th grade science."

And then— well, there is this look that happens. They try to hide it, but I have come to recognize it. My husband calls it the look of universal disdain. It flashes quickly across her face and the face of anyone in our line who happens to be listening. It remains for the briefest of instants, a micro-expression that includes pity and sympathy, rounded out by a final note of disgust.

"Oh well, bless yer soul, hon. Really—God bless ya for doing that job. Lord knows we need more great teachers. I could never even imagine teaching that age. Why, when my kids were that age, they were just monsters. Let me tell ya. Monsters."

Yes, honey, I believe you.

"My brother-in-law's uncle's sister, Rachel, why, she teaches kindergarten and she just LOVES those littles, ya know. They're just so CUTE."

Really? I am beginning to feel nauseous. I can't imagine teaching kindergarten; it's my worst nightmare. Well… that, and becoming an accountant.

"I just don't understand teenagers today, do you? They are just so DIFFICULT. How do y'all deal with those hormones in the classroom?"

At this point in the conversation, I start to zone out—a skill I learned, no doubt, from my 8th graders. While I agree with much of what she is saying in theory, my reality is much different than hers. I choose to teach 8th graders. I embrace their surliness. Their disrespectfulness. Their kindness. Their celebration of the underdog. Their leadership and strength. And, like all of us, their need for love and acceptance.

I take inventory of my snackage. In total: 18 donuts, 40 oats-and-honey granola bars, that large box of Goldfish crackers that will equal about 20 handfuls (more or less), and the jumbo-sized 80-piece bag of Jolly Ranchers. 158 snacks. I teach five classes of science five days per week. In a normal school year, I see about 140 students each day, so this means that in theory, each student will get one piece of snackage next week. The reality is, of course, that some students will get more and some none. Suddenly my amazing haul doesn't seem so elaborate.

At home, my mind flits back and forth in anticipation of the busy week ahead. I organize my class schedule and add an after-school meet-and-greet to my calendar. I re-check the outfit I picked out for tomorrow. I wrestle with a disparate array of thoughts and worries. When is Open House? Huh. I'm not sure. Did I remember to add the last granola bar to my lunch?

I struggle to fall asleep.

I am filled with hope and anxiety.

Tomorrow is the first day of school.

Michele M. Chamberlain

September: Days 1-18

Anticipation

Brring ... Brring!
My heart races as the morning bell rings for my first day of 8th grade.
Will my teachers like me? Will I have good classes? Do I look okay?
I hope I will find good, trusting friends.

I hope the teachers don't give too much homework or assign a big project on the first week.

I hope it will be a great year.

Kiara M., 14

Day 2

Yesterday was a blur.

The first school day for my 8th graders means, for them, a late start of 12:05 p.m., followed by six brief 17-minutes classes. Yesterday was chaos.

Today is a real school day–a proper day with 58 minutes per class. I stand by my open door and greet my 3rd period students with an optimistic "good morning" and a smile. A big, hearty, welcoming smile. Teachers used to be told "don't smile until December"–which, of course, is complete bullshit. No one wants to be in a classroom with a teacher they think dislikes, or even hates, them. So, I smile. And I attempt to remember a few of their names as they walk past me, some greeting me with hesitant smiles.

"Brandon, right?" He nods in the affirmative and moves to his seat.

I recognize the girl behind him. "Kirsten?" She stares at me. There is a hopeful look in her eyes.

"Uhm... no, let me try again. Krysta?"

Damn, there are so many "K" names this year. I am never going to get this right.

"It's Kayla, Mrs. Chamberlain."

Oh yes, Kayla. She smiles at me. She is so tiny; petite with blond hair. Fragile. Her wispy voice seems to match her body.

Students continue to file past me while I stumble through their names and hope that my effervescent greeting and occasional handshake or high-five makes up for my inability to remember all 30 of their names from yesterday's 17-minute class period. I remembered four in a row: Ben, Skylar, Tristan, Josh. They smile politely and greet me with a collective, "Good Morning, Mrs. Chamberlain," as they try to squeeze through the doorframe together. There are always students whose names you learn right away. The kind ones. The cheerful ones. The students who walk past me refusing to smile or even acknowledge my presence. I always pay attention to students who sit by themselves or refuse any overtures of kindness or attention. And of course, I can't help but notice the surly rulebreakers.

"Really?" I'll ask them. "It's the first day of school. Is this how you want to begin our year together? Hmmm?"

Yesterday in my 6th period class, there was a boy who got sick and started throwing up. It was awful for both of us. His family just immigrated from Somalia. A young boy named Abdullah. He looked scared and understandably embarrassed as his body retched uncontrollably. He rushed for the door and paused with one hand on the doorknob while he vomited again. The most I could do was call the office for help. One ridiculous rule for teachers is that we can never, ever, under any circumstances, leave our students unattended. We can't take a potty break unless there is another adult in the room. Too many school districts have been successfully sued by parents whose students were injured when a teacher stepped out of the classroom. I knew I needed help.

I looked around and said, "Do I have anyone in class who isn't afraid of a little vomit?"

A boy from the back of the room stood up and walked quickly towards Abdullah.

"I have little brothers," he explained. "Don't worry, Mrs. Chamberlain. I will take care of him."

He walked toward the door where Abdullah was frozen in place and gently took him by the arm to guide him to the nurse's office. He snagged the garbage can on the way out. I stood there in awe, just watching him. Later, I found out his name is Jetmir—an Albanian name that means 'Gift of God.'

I knew I would not forget his name. Ever.

Twenty-nine students—17 boys and 12 girls—managed to make it back to the same seat they chose yesterday. I promised them on Day One they could choose to sit anywhere with the condition they stay there all week. Throughout the day, students looked at me in disbelief as if I'd broken some sacred ritual of the first day of school.

"Aren't we going to get assigned seats?" Brandon had quipped yesterday.

"We'll see," I answered, smiling. "Don't worry about assigned seats today."

I never bother assigning seats or creating a seating chart during the first week of school because I don't know anything about my students yet. Some of my classes never have assigned seats. They just don't need them. After today, I will know my students better, and by Friday I will be able to decide about seating charts. I use the week to watch and learn; it's a skillfully executed recon mission any military commander would be proud of on a speed-dating timeline.

I have one student missing: a boy named Micah. Brandon says he thinks Micah was switched to one of my afternoon classes. I grab a sticky note from my desk to remind myself to check the online attendance rosters. By the end of the day, my desk will be covered with sticky notes in a variety of sizes and colors to signal their importance. Yellow means "take care of this RIGHT NOW" and the pink ones are just little reminders for me. Green stickies mean an email or phone call home. After a dozen years in the classroom, this is the fastest and most efficient way for me to remember things. After 6th period ends, I will finally sit at my desk and attend to all the crises of the day until those sticky notes make their way into my trash bin and my desk is clear for tomorrow.

But we're not there yet. I still have a whole day ahead of me.

The class is quiet. My new students wait patiently to see what I have in store for them. Since this is only our first full day together, it is fair to say we are still in our honeymoon period–hence the quiet class. A student raises her hand. I see her and quickly check my notes for her name. "Yes, Izzie?"

"So, what are we doing today, Mrs. C?" She shortens my name to a single consonant.

"Oh, we are going to have some fun today!" My voice is bubbly ... maybe a little too bubbly. "I have a challenge for you and for the whole class. I will explain the directions in a minute."

She pauses. "Is this graded?"

"Well, do you think it needs to be graded?" I ask.

My question surprises her. I can see from the look on their faces that it surprises the rest of the class, too. I walk to the back of my room where the lab stations are already prepared with supplies: one meter of tape, a collection of plastic straws, and the instructions, complete with diagrams. Their eyes follow me as I move around the room. I hear some quiet talking and notice Izzie has started talking to her table partner. There are a few other talkers too. I can't begin to explain the directions until I have everyone's attention. So, I wait. Our school has a universal hand signal that means, "Sit up straight, eyes on the speaker, mouths off". I put my hand up and wait for the class to settle. It doesn't happen right away. I stand still. I wait.

Finally, silence.

"Thank you for giving me your attention. Today you will divide up into groups of two, three, or four people. You can be in any group you choose."

More surprised looks. I am sure they are wondering, "Is this teacher stupid? Or crazy? Why would she let us divide up into any groups we want? Doesn't she know we will just hang with our friends?"

I continue. "The object of today's challenge is to build a straw tower using only the materials you have at your lab table. The tower that cantilevers off the edge of the table the furthest, without dipping below the edge of the tabletop, wins. Does anyone know what it means to cantilever?"

Ben raises his hand to explain. He's got to be a future engineer, for sure.

After five or six minutes of discussion and questions, we finish reviewing the directions and students are ready to begin the challenge. But it's not their engineering skills I am really interested in. I create this event so I can take a snapshot of their behavior and social pecking order. Who are the class leaders? Who are the risk takers? Do I have anyone who cannot work in a team situation? What can I learn about my new class in the 30 minutes it takes to build these straw towers?

"Are there any final questions about this challenge activity?" I glance around the room. The class is still. No one raises a hand.

"Okay—one final little bit I forgot to mention. Each member of the winning team will earn a donut."

I put a tray of four donuts on the table in front of me. Suddenly the mood of the classroom changes. I watch them sit up a little straighter and they begin to motion to their friends.

I hear comments like, "What? No way!! We can get donuts?"

Tristan shouts out excitedly, "Our group is going to win for sure, Mrs. Chamberlain!" He and Ben high-five each other.

Someone yells, "Is there anything for 2nd place?"

This is exactly the reaction I was waiting for. NOW they are ready.

The room is buzzing. It's time to get this show on the road.

"Remember, you have 30 minutes to complete this challenge. Get ready to divide into groups. Ready, set, and ... GO!"

I stand back and watch. I take mental notes about my students—no clipboards or writing, because kids tend to worry about what I am writing instead of focusing on their group. A student named Jamal is organizing his team. He manages them like the captain of a football team, giving quick directions and assigning tasks. He has brought over some notebook paper so he can illustrate his idea to the group. Izzie has already started constructing a tower with her team, and she talks them through her idea. I can see that she has convinced them that her idea will work.

Brandon is sitting on the lab table, watching his team. I glide over to where he is sitting and lean in, so I can whisper in his ear, "Please don't sit on the lab tables." He complies but as soon as I move to the next team he hops back on. I turn around and address him, more firmly the second time. "Brandon, I need you to not sit on the lab table." This time he stays off.

I grab a sticky note and write "safety contracts" on it, and when I am close enough to my desk, I add it to the growing line of color near my keyboard. Brandon's team is struggling to begin. I go over and ask them to tell me their ideas. I ask them, "How do you think you should begin building a tower? Would you start at the top or the bottom?" My ridiculous question propels them forward as they try to show me their fledgling plan. I eavesdrop on their conversations while they work. I smile encouragingly as I walk from one lab table to another.

We have a lot of work ahead of us.

It is amazing how much you can learn in 30 minutes.

Day 10

The honeymoon is over, at least in 5th period.

Today is our second official Friday of the school year. Friday afternoons can be tough times in middle school. With 180 school days per year, there are theoretically 36 Fridays. But of course, that doesn't account for long weekends, conferences, holidays, and snow days, where Fridays are eliminated from the week. I subtract, and then decide on a nice round number, 30. Thirty total Fridays in the school year, minus last week and today. 28 dreaded Fridays left.

It's always a little tougher for me to teach my afternoon classes, not because they are more unruly or needier, but rather because my patience is worn thin by the time the bell rings at 12:17 p.m., marking the start of my afternoon session. I've already spent three hours on the front lines– a teaching marathon punctuated by tiny three-minute breaks every hour. I think back to my days of office work, before I became a teacher, and remember we took 10-minute breaks every hour, drawing out our breaks with hushed conversations around the coffee maker. I long for a chance to grab a cup of coffee or catch up with a coworker. My desk is already covered with stickies. I don't have enough time between classes to go to the bathroom. I can barely catch my breath, because as soon as the last student exits the back door of the classroom, I am busy greeting my next group as they enter the front door. Eighty-three students in and out of my room before lunch. Before the bathroom. Before a few precious moments of quiet.

Lunch is over. Fifth period students begin to trickle into class, but they don't settle. There are still five or six students milling around in the hallway when the final bell rings, including Micah. I take attendance, hoping the extra 30 seconds or so will give them time to find their seats. They are 8th graders. They know they should be in their seats.

Micah casually wanders to an open seat. Not his seat. An open seat. Mariah darts in quickly and sits down next to Faith. Her eyes apologize for being late.

There are still three outside the door. I decide on a public service announcement.

"Ladies and Gentlemen, everyone should now be in their seat. I need you to have your notebooks and pencils out. Let's read the warmup together."

15

Notebooks appear, along with a few pencils. I wait for the chattering to die down. Faith and Mariah are ready. They are sitting quietly together, pencils in hand. Mariah is doodling on the cover of her notebook.

"Hi Faith!". She smiles. "Would you be comfortable reading the warmup out loud for the class?" Some students hate reading out loud. In middle school, it's not about the ability to read, but the confidence to do so. I give her an out just in case. She doesn't take it. It's a good sign.

As Faith reads, it feels like the class is getting ready to settle, like we are almost to that magical tipping point where the students are focused and ready to learn and I have their complete attention. As Faith finishes reading, my shoulders relax a little. I didn't realize they were so tense until just now. I open my mouth and a word pops out just as the door opens. Michael and Jasper enter with Kailee behind them (I think it is Kailee... I'm still having a hard time keeping all the "K" names in order). She slides into the room just as the door is closing, and hands me her note. I glance down at it long enough to see that her name is spelled K-a-y-l-e-e. Fine. Michael has a note, too, that he plops down on my desk before he heads slowly to his seat, offering high-fives along the way. He smiles at me as he finally sits, a big goofy smile that says, "Aren't you glad I made it to class today?" He's not a bad kid; he's a disrupter. I smile back at him.

He doesn't have any supplies—no notebook, no pencil. Nothing. Nada. Shit. Didn't he just come from the counselor's office? What the hell were they thinking sending him to class with no supplies? I grab an extra notebook and pencil, and head back to his seat to get him started on our warmup. By now, the class is chatty, and only a handful of students have started working on the question that Faith read out loud a minute ago. I give the class signal: the raised hand that means, "Please be quiet and give me your attention". At least, that's what it meant two class periods ago. Right now, it feels more optional than absolute. The hand signal isn't working. Michael is charmingly distracting a girl who sits in front of him, and the noise level in the class begins to escalate. It is at this exact moment that Jasper, who has been hovering by the door, decides to make his grand entrance. With the class teetering on chaos, I calmly ask Jasper for his note. "Don't got one," he replies as he brushes past me.

I watch him as he shuffles toward his desk. As he passes by classmates, he firmly smacks them on the back of the head, one by one. For a moment, I am mesmerized. Stunned. *Is he actually hitting people on the head?* The shrieks and complaints that follow rouse me from my stupor and I jump into action. I manage to intercept Jasper just as he prepares one final onslaught of smacking. I muster up my calmest, most sincere teacher voice.

"Jasper," I begin, "it is not okay to hit or touch other people. I need you to leave my class and head down to the office."

His voice rises above the calamity as he shouts at me, "What the fuck?" and in protest he adds, "I didn't even do anything."

As he exits the class, I hear Micah shout, "Stay strong, brother."

I glance at the clock and realize that I've lost four minutes of class time. Four precious instructional minutes. If I had this much disruption every day in 5th period, I would lose 12 hours of class time over the course of the school year. I know classes with behavior problems struggle academically. It's my job to figure out how to get this class on track and help them become successful learners. I don't have the answers today.

As I move back to the front of the classroom, I begin the process of refocusing the class. I grab a small handful of Jolly Ranchers, and as I repeat the warmup question out loud, I set a timer for two minutes and project it on the overhead, so everyone can see it. "Okay, in two minutes I am going to call on a few of you to share out your ideas with the class." I place the treats on my demonstration counter where everyone can see them. "Ready, set, GO!" The conversations resume, but now most of them are focused on the warmup. While they are working, I rush to my desk. One yellow sticky. One green sticky. A quick call to the office to let them know Jasper is on his way. When I call, our head secretary asks when I will be sending the required written discipline referral. I jot down "referral Jasper" on another yellow sticky. One more thing to take care of after school today. The timer tells me I have 45 seconds left to walk around the classroom and preview student ideas before I call on anyone. This preview time is essential: it guides my questions; lets me know which students understand the content; and shows me where the disconnects and misconceptions are happening. This is what I should have been doing the entire time.

Twelve minutes of the class period gone. Forty-six minutes to go. We still have a quiz to take, and I am not sure I have enough energy to keep the class together. Teaching is exhausting business.

I take a deep breath and let it out slowly as I begin calling on random students. Forty-five minutes to go.

Day 17

Dear Mrs. Chamberlain,

Thank you for being such a great teacher. I was so happy when I got my schedule this year and saw your name.

You are a really fun teacher.

I didn't like science last year, but I hope I will like it with you. See you in 3rd period.

Your student,

Kayla

It's 6:12 a.m.

Kayla's note greets me as I turn the key to my classroom door. I remember that Kayla is the petite blond who was shy, with a hesitant smile. I see the card—hand drawn with purple hearts around the edges—peeping out from the bottom of my door. She somehow managed to leave it between the time I left school yesterday and this morning. Despite the early hour and the fact I've only half-finished my first cup of coffee, her thoughtful gesture leaves a big toothy smile on my face. As I get to my desk, I stop to reread her note, and am stuck on the line, "I didn't like science last year." Her words stick in my brain and I can't shake them off, even as I finish some mundane tasks and drink the rest of my coffee.

Experience reminds me it could be a wide variety of non-science memories that would cause a student like Kayla to develop negative feelings about a previous class—a personality conflict with the teacher, social situations, bullying—things that have nothing to do with science but could skew her impressions of the class. Still, I am worried. I want her to have a good year with me. I want to change her impressions of science, yes; but more importantly, I want to help Kayla feel empowered as a student.

An article I wrote in 2018 for an online national teaching blog addressed this very subject: the disenfranchisement of young girls in science, technology, engineering, and math (STEM) fields. When I was researching for this article, I discovered in the United States, young girls develop negative feelings about math and science as early as 2nd grade, despite their success on standardized tests that clearly show subject aptitude. This really shocked me. Second grade? That is so young to develop negative feelings towards anything, really. Men and women graduate in roughly equal proportions in STEM fields, but men end up working (and building successful careers) in STEM fields at a much higher percentage than women, particularly in areas like computer science and engineering. While there are many societal issues that influence career choice and success, I think these early negative impressions of science and STEM are a fundamental reason we fail to fill our STEM pipeline. Nations like China, India, Germany, Finland—in fact, most other industrialized nations—don't have the same issues we have engaging women in successful STEM-related careers. The results from these countries speak for themselves, and I can't help but constantly question our Americanized approach to education.

Kayla's note draws me back to my preparations for today. It's a Tuesday, so that means most students will be here. There seem to be a lot of absences on

Fridays, and in this school district, our late-start Wednesdays tend to be days when students sleep in a little too much or skip school entirely. I can't change what occurs outside of the walls of my classroom; I can only offer a more attractive alternative: a robust and fulfilling environment that challenges students while supporting their individual needs. A place where they are emotionally safe, where they are always welcome. Kayla's note reminds me to pay attention to relationship building, which is probably the most important thing teachers can do to ensure the future success of our students. If students feel a connection with me, and with the larger classroom community, they are much more likely to engage, to show determination, to persevere towards excellence. Relationships are essential. They are the only genuine predictor of student success.

The warm-up question I prepared earlier this morning for 8th grade science class now seems out of place. I'm not sure my kids need more science right now. My gut tells me to switch gears. With a quick highlight and touch of the 'delete' key, the misguided warm-up is gone. Time for a do-over.

I have an hour to prepare since first period is my planning time. For now, time is my friend. I grab a pack of sticky notes from my collection and begin writing short, personal messages to each student. For Kayla I write, "I enjoy seeing your big, beautiful smile each morning," but then rip that one up and start over. Kayla doesn't need me to tell her she has a great smile or how much I enjoy it. She needs to hear she is valued as a student—for her effort and contributions to the class. This time I write, "Kayla, your warm-up answers yesterday really showed me how much effort you are willing to put into this class. Thank you for your hard work!"

Some of the notes are easier to write than others. Brandon has been a tough customer since the first day of school. He is testing the boundaries. I can tell he is smart and capable—even funny at times—but being naughty seems like a role he adopted some time ago and he can't quite let go of it. On his note I write, "I really appreciate your wittiness and fun humor" and I hope my note rings true enough that he accepts the compliment. Tristan has been quiet and a little moody the past few days. I'm not sure what is going on. Maybe he will tell me. Most of the time he has this warm, effusive personality, and he is an extremely competent leader. I think back to the Tristan I observed during our engineering challenge. He and his partner Ben won. Their design was so good that it was the grand winner out of all four classes. I decide to write on his note, "Your leadership has a positive and powerful effect on everyone you meet." It is difficult to tap into truly genuine compliments for each member of the class, so I try to imagine them for one moment (from the past 17 days) where they did something, or wrote something, or acted in a way that was positive and memorable. Reminiscing about the first three weeks of class helps me zip through the next batch of compliments.

I have two more notes left to write and I am stuck. A girl named Nicole has hardly been here for the first three weeks of school. I feel like I barely know her; I want her compliment to be sincere. Finally, I write "Nicole, I am looking forward to getting to know you better. I am so glad you are in my class this year."

One left. I need to write a genuine compliment for Izzie, and I just can't summon one. I saved her note for last, hoping I would locate just one positive memory so I could construct a meaningful note for her. We've had a rough start together. She is so bright, so capable; it breaks my heart to watch her self-sabotage. Her behavior in my class is far outside the norm of what I've come to expect from middle school girls. Izzie is hostile, even aggressive. She rebukes any attempt at praise or compliments and brushes off any hint of success as a 'mistake.' She wants to stir the pot, and she is damn good at it. This has become her identity. When I've tried to ignore or gloss over her behavior, she will call me on it.

"I know you are pissed, Mrs. C. Doesn't it make you mad when I break pencils in your class and throw them on the floor?" Her jagged comments are always followed by an eerie smile or triumphant smirk. Of the past 17 class days, she's been tardy 14 times. I've called home and left messages. I've sent emails. I've called from my cellphone at odd hours just in case her parents have learned to screen calls coming from the school. I've had no luck with parent contact so far. There is an old address in her file, but not a current one. I heard her family was living with friends for a few months last year. I wonder if they have landed in a new home. I make a note on a sticky to check with the office about an updated address. I've heard rumors about some rough times in elementary school. Life has been a harsh teacher. Not an excuse, but it explains a lot.

Three minutes to go.

I close my eyes and rewind memories in my mind's eye, perusing our day-to-day interactions to find just one moment I can use to write a genuinely positive comment. And suddenly there it is, buried under a litany of kind rebukes and redirection. I write quickly and save the note to stick under her seat.

As my 3rd period classes enter, I hand each student a blank sticky note and remind them to read today's warm-up question. From the corner of my eye, I watch as students retrieve the messages hidden under their seats. Their surprised looks reshape into little half-smiles. I try to give them privacy to enjoy the notes by busying myself taking attendance and sharpening a few pencils. The warm-up question directs them to write an anonymous compliment and deliver that note sometime today. The classroom is silent except for the occasional shuffle of a chair or a hand quickly brushing eraser crumbs off the desk.

The day is over, finally.

I head to my desk. I don't sit down a lot during the day. I can't teach science while I am sitting.

My classroom has hard concrete floors—not carpet, like most classrooms. My feet are tired. My test for a good pair of shoes is whether they can survive an entire day on these unforgiving floors. This pair cannot. I kick them off into the garbage and grab the slippers hidden under my desk. It feels good to sit.

I begin wading through the line of colorful stickies near my keyboard and see two yellow ones crumpled up under my desk. I unfold the first one, which has a half-completed game of tic-tac-toe.

Huh. Well, it's a start.

I open the second note, and I'm surprised to see the message I wrote for Izzie: "You have a group of kind and loyal friends, and that tells me that you must be a good friend, too."

On the back of the note she has written, "Thank you."

October: Days 19-40

Digging In

The difference between a good teacher and a great teacher is a small one, albeit one of the key differences that truly separates the normal typical teacher from the memorable, amazing ones. This difference is the teacher's attitude, passion, and approach to the subject.

A student can always tell, right away when they walk through the door on the first day of school, if that teacher will be exciting or boring. And life's all about those first impressions. I've seen the difference this sort of mentality a teacher has for a subject make on a classroom.

Michael S., 14

Day 21

I t's a Def Leppard kind of Monday.

The 8th grade hallway doors open at 7:10 a.m., and on Mondays one of my extra duties is to greet students. It's another chance to make connections with my kids. I look forward to seeing them on Monday mornings.

I blast classic rock from the speakers in my classroom as I get ready to unlock the hallway doors. My classroom is near these doors that mark the entrance to 8th grade territory. I turn the music up until the noise is almost unbearable inside my room. The speakers crackle just a little, so I dial the volume back until the crackling stops. The resonant sounds of Joe Elliott singing "Pour Some Sugar on Me" fills the hallways. Since this is public school, and most of my students' parents are the same age I am, I feel assured I am not violating anyone's sensibilities with my music choices. I am sure they have heard worse.

Dan, one of our math teachers, bustles by me as I push the doors open. He cocks his head to listen, and then nods with approval. His eyes twinkle warmly as he heads down the end of the hall towards his room. Most mornings, Dan wanders the hallway with his guitar, playing riffs and brief ditties, sometimes stopping near a locker to serenade a particularly cranky student. I've heard from his students he will even sing about geometry formulas or the Pythagorean theorem. Dan teaches advanced math classes for our highly capable students. He has this easy style that lightens the mood in the hallway. I don't think our students know how lucky they are to have him as a teacher. I see him at the end of the hallway with his guitar, making his usual rounds. His passion is contagious, and I kick up my greetings a bit. I put my hands up to pass out some high-fives. I can't help but dance a little as the song finishes, and "Pyromania" begins. I don't mind looking a little silly in front of my students. It makes me more human. A few of them give me awkward smiles as they pass by, but most of them are just too tired to enjoy the spectacle I am making of myself.

7:10 a.m. is too damn early for school.

Half-open eyes peer out from underneath tightened hoodies, and a few students are slurping coffee or energy drinks as they meander down the hall. Their shoulders are hunched—not so much from the weight of their backpacks but from sheer exhaustion. From my vantage point, I watch them unload backpacks and disappear down the back stairs at the end of the hall. I wish I could turn them around and send them home for a few more hours of sleep Selfishly, I am glad I don't have a 1st period class. My students are barely awake when they arrive to 2nd period, so I imagine any earlier they would appear comatose.

The raucous music of Def Leppard that was once nearing dangerous decibels has been absorbed by soft coats and warm bodies. The sounds emerging from the hallway resemble a layer of overtones. I can't distinguish one conversation from another—just the high and low pitches that bizarrely fit together to create a chord-like structure. It's the sound of Monday mornings.

The hallway begins to empty and a student rushes by me in a whir, his lanky 6-foot frame ping-ponging off the lockers, his arms flailing in the air as he knocks into classmates. Bystanders quickly veer out of his way to avoid immediate impact. There is some yelling and I hear a few swear words and loud bangs. I don't think he means to really hurt them, but he can't stop himself.

When he finally sees me, he greets me with a loud-but-charming, "Heeeyyy, Mrs. Chamberlain!"

I realize this is Micah, my student from 5th period. His smile is disarmingly charismatic. He spins around in the middle of the hallway, pirouetting out of control as he heads back towards me. The hall between us is now completely empty, and I walk toward him with my hands up, signaling him to slow down before he crashes. He manages to stop his body right in front of me, and although his feet have paused, his body is still wiggling; his arms are unable to hang quietly at his side and he moves his head as if he is being distracted by some ultrasonic whistle.

"Hey Micah, it's great to see you!" I try to make eye contact with him, but he can't seem to focus his head into one spot long enough to meet my gaze. "Where are you headed?" He looks confused. "Where's your class?"

"Uh... here... right... here," he stammers.

I can't quite understand what he's saying.

"Your class is up here, in this hallway?" I counter. He nods and points to the room right across from mine, our 8th grade interventions classroom.

I move closer to him and offer to escort him to class, but he isn't ready.

"I gotta get a drink," he states, as he darts away from me and further down the hall to the water fountains.

I stay in the hallway and wait for him to finish, then wait for him to bounce and take a final spin into the room.

"See you 5th!" he shouts as the door closes behind him.

Micah has ADHD, as well as learning disabilities.

ADHD (attention deficit hyperactivity disorder) is a mental health issue that often affects learning. Statistically, boys are three times more likely than girls to be diagnosed with ADHD; but oddly, the propensity for diagnosis changes depending on the state in which you live—from a low of 5% to a high of 14%. It's unclear if this variance in diagnosis is because some states have healthier, less affected children, or rather (and more likely), some states have less access to health care. If you are a white male, there is a significant chance you will experience some form of ADHD during your lifetime. The fortunate ones are diagnosed early—in 2nd or 3rd grade—before their unsuccessful attempts at learning become hardwired and repeated failure permanently destroys, or at least maligns, their self-esteem.

Back in my own classroom, I grab my special education binder—a notebook that lists all my students who are in special education, and I flip through until I find Micah's individual education plan, or IEP: a document that details both his learning disabilities and his treatment plan. The papers I have are incomplete and only give a brief summary of classroom interventions. There is neither a history of diagnosis nor a description of any medications he should be taking. His dramatic performance in the hallway earlier made it apparent to me he is currently unmedicated. It is unfortunate, but not uncommon, for middle school students to suddenly go off their medication or refuse to take it, and I wonder if this is Micah's choice or his parents'. Sometimes parents will give their students 'medication holidays' during the school year (or refuse medication completely) because many ADHD medications can interfere with growth or delay the start of puberty. I understand the choice, but I am not sure if parents understand the dramatic difference medication makes for their child (or other children) at school, where they are required to sit still and pay attention hour after hour. Our school system rewards the attentive and quiet student—not a student like Micah, who ping-pongs his way from class to class. I keep the spaces in the back corners of my classroom free of desks, so students on 'holiday' can bounce or run in place, because they literally cannot stop their bodies from moving. It's sad to watch. When they cannot focus, they cannot learn.

It's that simple.

I check my calendar. Micah and his family have an IEP meeting scheduled for later in the week. This is a re-evaluation of his progress, goals, and skills. I leave myself a pink sticky as a reminder; I don't want to get caught up with another crisis and miss this opportunity to meet with them. They need to know Micah is a good kid. He has a certain kindness and charm about him that is easy to love. He can't control his behavior, I know, but it doesn't make it any less frustrating for me. I have an entire class of students to teach, and 5th period is showing the predictable signs of strain from Micah's minute-by-minute disruptions. And he isn't alone. Jasper and Michael add their own brand of trouble to the class. Fifth period has a completely different vibe on days when any of those three is absent. I shouldn't be happy on those days, and I feel guilty that I am. It's not fair that one class has so many behavior issues. One, I could deal with; three has become a nightmare. It's not their fault they were shoved into the same class together. No, that was someone else's brilliant idea.

I want to have a real conversation with Micah's parents. He needs me to be a great teacher for him, a strong advocate … but right now, I am not sure how I can be. He needs me to be his champion in this meeting; but I have been warned to be careful what I say or imply about his ADHD, even though it is a documented medical condition. I cannot insinuate his behavior might be connected to his lack of regular medication. I am not legally allowed to suggest his school life would be more productive or more successful if he weren't bouncing off the walls all day or slamming students into lockers.

Only the facts, please. We don't want to overwhelm the parents with too much information.

Maybe they need to feel a little overwhelmed.

I sure as hell do.

Day 32

have a favorite class. I know I am not supposed to, but I can't help it.

I start my teaching day during 2nd period with Environmental Science, a class I had the opportunity to design and write last summer. Maybe I love this class so intensely because I have so much of my heart and soul invested. I spent dozens of hours researching state and national standards and then writing a template for the class, called a framework, that had to be approved by our state office of education before it could officially become a class. I designed each unit, each project, and each field experience. This class is my baby.

There are only 24 students this semester—a small group compared to my normal 30. Students who take this class don't have any special talents in science, per se, but they tend to be more successful in this type of class because it is project-based and team-oriented. Their emerging advocacy for all things environmental is inspiring. Over the past six weeks, this class has developed into a tight-knit community.

Have I mentioned how much I love this class?

Today we are going outside to conduct a field investigation on different types of pollution sources. It is a beautiful October morning—a little chilly, but the sun is peeking through. I can't wait for 2nd period, so we can get started. I watch the clock anxiously as the minutes tick away.

Ira opens the classroom door and rushes in, apologizing for arriving later than he had planned and completely disregarding the 50 or more minutes of soul-crushing traffic he must endure in order to volunteer in my classroom once a week. Ira retired several years ago as the chief pathologist at a large, local medical center in the region. We had been friends for a number of years, and he had occasionally visited my science classes as a guest presenter. When the time came for him to consider retirement, we had a long conversation about his desire to volunteer more regularly in my science classes and how he could best make an impact. I told him I wanted him working in the classroom, with students, not designing bulletin boards or correcting papers. I asked him if he knew what he was getting himself into, volunteering to work with young teens; and I warned him that during the first few weeks he would leave my class feeling exhausted, beaten, and like he had just run a marathon.

"You know, Michele," he answered, "If I can reach just one student–if I can make a connection and help one young person because of the time I spend in your classroom–then all of the effort will be worth it. Maybe I save a few starfish."

"A few what?"

So, he explains the starfish story, one I haven't heard, about a man wandering along the beach among millions of starfish that have washed ashore. The man sees a young girl reaching down and grabbing starfish, one at a time, throwing them back into the ocean. He approaches the girl and asks, "Why are you doing this? Look at all these starfish. You can't possibly make a difference!" The girl bends down, picks up another starfish, tosses it into the surf, and looks back up at the man before exclaiming confidently, "Made a difference to that one!"

For the past three years, Ira and I have spent every Tuesday side by side, wrangling 8th graders. His extreme attention to detail and borderline obsessive perfectionism is the perfect complement to my big-picture mindset and ethereal creativity. We have different styles, but it is a perfect partnership. He reaches students that I cannot. They call him Dr. Allen. I call him my friend.

We wait together for the bell that will usher in our students. We exchange pleasantries as we wait; but really, we are both excited for the same thing: to get started with the business of teaching our students.

McKay and Mattias enter first. "Hey, Dr. Allen–you're here!" they exclaim in unison. They offer me a "Good morning, Mrs. C," but I've learned over the years of working with Ira that Tuesdays belong to him. This is his one day to build stronger relationships with our students and make real connections. Sammie walks in next. She smiles coyly and chimes in, "It must be Tuesday today because Dr. Allen is here!" A friendly parade of students fills the room with similar greetings. Clarissa, Camden, Riley, Austin, and Gabriella are all in this class. I feel fortunate to get them for a coveted two hours a day: one hour now, and one hour later in my regular science classes. Casey, a student I taught last year in one of my rare 7th grade classes, is here too. I see Gabriella's best friend, Victoria.

As Ira finishes greeting the last swarm of students, I open my mouth to remind them to get their boots on, but my words are too late. Everyone is ready to go outside, and the bell hasn't rung yet. Riley has his video camera to record our session today and create a class video. Camden is helping him and carrying a microphone. My team leaders, Victoria, Gabriella, Mattias, and Cooper, already have their groups together. McKay has on hip waders to muck around in our local wetland and collect water samples for future testing. Ira grabs a pair of rubber boots so he can demonstrate collection techniques for McKay.

We head out, and I exit the classroom last to lock the door. As I follow behind them, I listen to their excited murmurings. I admire the collegiate attitude of this class and the warm environment we've been able to establish in a mere six weeks. It is a model class—the kind I wish I were able to build every year but haven't always done successfully. Every class has its own unique personality, and some become bogged down in the negative. Sometimes just one person can tip a class or change the way the group functions. I am aware of how quickly the temperature of a class can change, so I feel truly blessed with a class like this.

We arrive at the wetlands, a federally protected area that borders our school grounds. The team leaders are busy discussing pollution sources with their groups. Everyone here knows their role and purpose. Riley is starting his video work, and he and Camden wander a bit from the group to get a good angle shot. McKay carefully wades out into the water with Ira next to him. They both look so serious; McKay is listening intently to Ira explain the intricacies of water collection. I have a supporting role in this unfolding story; my students take the lead and make it clear they don't need further direction from me. I have a few seconds to watch some birds at the far end of the wetland, appreciating the little mental break in the middle of all this busyness.

I am interrupted by the crackling of my walkie-talkie. I always carry one when we work outside.

"Chamberlain?" A pause. "Chamberlain, where is your class located?"

"We're out past the tennis courts, working in the wetlands," I reply.

"Okay. Sending a student out to you now."

"What?" I am confused. All my students are here today.

"You have a new student joining your class. We'll send her out right now."

I walk to the edge of the tennis courts, closer to the school, so she can see me. As she rounds the corner, I see immediately my "new" student is Izzie.

Oh, no way. No. No. No. Shit.

I struggle to keep my feelings under control. Things between us haven't been much better, despite her "thank you" on the crumpled sticky note she left under the desk for me two weeks ago. Outwardly, she is still hostile—perhaps slightly less than before. Two hours a day with a student who actively dislikes me. Great. The addition of Izzie will cause a rebalancing—a shifting of roles and attitudes—

that could go badly unless I am super proactive and positive. I have about eight seconds to get my own attitude under control before Izzie is close enough to hear my greeting. She is already an expert at ferreting out bullshit. I must be sincere.

"Hi Izzie!"

She nods in my direction and extends her arm just close enough that I can grab the note that balances on her fingertips.

"What class are you transferring from?" I ask.

"Choir," she replies without explanation. I am sure I will find out more of this story later.

"Okay. Well, right now we are out by the wetlands area collecting data. Why don't you follow me, and I'll take you over there."

She's wearing old white tennis shoes—not exactly the best thing for being outside near a wetland. Transferring into this class probably wasn't her idea, either.

When we arrive at the edge of the work area, the teams are wrapping up their data collection and Ira and McKay have finished collecting their water samples. I give the signal and have the class gather around. With as much enthusiasm as I can muster, I introduce Izzie to the class.

"Izzie, I am going to assign you a team for right now, so you can learn about today's field activity and data collection." I glance over at Gabriella. "Gabriella, Izzie is going to join your team today. When we get back to our room, I will be over to work with your team." Gabriella nods, and seems nonplussed by her new addition.

As we head back inside, Izzie lags behind the group. I stay back with her and let Ira lead the class back to school. Izzie and I walk side by side, but we are not together.

A highway of silence separates us until Izzie crosses it as she says, "Mrs. C, I don't want to work with a group. I can do the field report. Just give me the notes and I will do the work by myself."

I control my impulse to give her the party line about how this is a team-oriented class and scientists don't work by themselves. My words will only further the divide between us. She doesn't want to be in this class any more than I want her there.

I stop walking. "Izzie, I understand joining this class was probably not your choice. You probably don't know anyone in here, and I understand you are feeling uncomfortable being forced to join a group. Will you let Dr. Allen work with you today to get you caught up?"

She jumps at the opportunity, and a glimmer of surprise sweeps across her face. She was ready for a fight and didn't get one.

Ira has already anticipated my plan and invites Izzie to sit with him in the classroom. They sit in the back, heads together, working quietly for the remainder of the class period. Before the bell rings, Izzie has shared most of a completed field report on her Google drive.

It is impressive work for her first day of class. In fact, it's the best work she's done in the past six weeks.

Ira has found his starfish.

November: Days 41- 60

A Dose of Reality

Dear Ms. Avila,
    My name is Michele Chamberlain, and I am your niece Amanda's 8th grade science teacher.

I wanted to contact you regarding a recent assignment that Amanda completed in class–a short research essay about famous scientists.

Unfortunately, it appears she plagiarized her entire essay directly from two internet sources. As I am sure you know, copying someone else's work is a violation of our student code of conduct, and is considered cheating.

Amanda will be offered an opportunity to redo this assignment. She has two weeks to complete this redo assignment. She can earn full credit if she follows the guidelines of the assignment.

In the meantime, the gradebook will reflect a "0" grade.

Please feel free to contact me with any questions or concerns.

With kind regards,

Michele Chamberlain, NBCT, Science

Day 45

My phone is ringing.

I can hear it as I walk toward my room. I've been at the copier, printing out grade reports.

Friday is the official end of the first academic quarter, so today is a dedicated grading day for teachers and a late-start day for students. They won't arrive until 9:50 a.m.–2nd period–so I have plenty of time to focus and wrap up a few comments and tasks.

I reach my desk and grab the receiver just in time.

"This is Michele. Oh, hi Patty!" Patty is our building head secretary.

"Hi Michele! Hey, I need to schedule a parent meeting. Is today good–around 2:30 p.m.?

I take a quick look at my calendar. "Sure, Patty. Today after school is fine. Can you give me some details? Who are we meeting with?"

"We had a call from Ms. Avila. She wants to meet to discuss an assignment that her niece completed for your class. She called the office very, very upset about your email accusing her niece of cheating. Also, can you drop by the office with the paper Amanda wrote and all your notes? Doug wants to look at them before the meeting."

Doug is our principal.

"Sure, Patty, I'll be right down."

I can hear a click as she hangs up the phone, but I hold onto the receiver for a moment. My heart sinks. This is going to be a difficult meeting, and I need to be as prepared as possible. I grab the folder where I've kept Amanda's essay along with the multitude of documents I've printed containing her plagiarized paragraphs, now highlighted in yellow. This isn't a case of a student not understanding the difference between paraphrasing and plagiarism, or some stolen sentences here and there interspersed with a thoughtfully written sentence or two. This was blatant and intentional cheating. I have my evidence carefully organized as I head downstairs.

Doug is in his office when I arrive, and he smiles and waves me inside. He stands up and moves from behind his desk to meet me halfway. His smile is warm and genuine, and the corners of his eyes crinkle up a little as he meets my gaze.

"It's great to see you, Michele! Thanks for taking a moment stop by!" He is so cheerful and casual; I wonder for a split second if he remembers why I've been summoned to his office.

"So, I just got off the phone with Ms. Avila. Her niece"—he pauses here— "what's her name? Amanda, I think? She is in your 6th period class?"

"Yes, Doug, that's correct."

"She is pretty upset. She says you accused her niece of cheating on an assignment. Can you tell me more about that? His voice is calm, and he is still smiling his warm smile. I relax a bit. I know he is giving me the benefit of the doubt.

I open the folder and start presenting the evidence—sort of a pretrial run-through with a kindly defense attorney. "Here is the paper Amanda wrote, Doug. And you can see by the corresponding highlights the areas where the paper has been copied, word for word, from two specific sources."

The room is quiet as he peruses the documents carefully and contemplates the scope of the violation. I wait.

It's a short wait. He finishes his assessment and closes the folder.

"Yep, you're right. I knew you would be. Good work getting all of this organized so thoroughly. This will really help us clear things up." He pauses. "Ms. Avila was absolutely insistent there was no way possible her niece would have cheated on this assignment. She was so vehement on the phone. I wanted to take a moment to touch base with you just in case there was any chance of a misunderstanding. And there isn't. I absolutely agree with your decision, Michele. Again, good job on being so thorough. See you this afternoon, then?"

He ushers me out the door with the same warm inviting presence as when I came in, that makes this feel like a meeting of old chums than a serious tête-à-tête.

Relief and frustration confront me simultaneously as I leave Doug's office and head back to my room. I am relieved I haven't made some terrible error that would require hours of discussion and apology and the subsequent humiliation that comes with poor decision making. But I am more relieved to know my principal has my back going into this afternoon's meeting. Truth be told, he has always had my back—even when I was a first-year teacher and made those colossal first-year teacher mistakes that required him to apologize on my behalf and issue a stern warning later. I appreciate working for a principal who cares deeply about his staff and always takes the time to listen first. Some of my colleagues at other schools have not been so fortunate.

And my frustration? There are no winners here today. It doesn't matter that I have Amanda dead to rights. If our relationship is damaged, it is my responsibility to repair it, which could take months—perhaps the rest of the school year. Amanda has done well in my 6th period science class to date. She is bright and capable, and she always brings a positive energy that persists to the end of the day. She is involved in a number of extracurriculars, including dance and volleyball. Her home life has been challenging in the past but seems to be smoother now that she is living with her aunt. More than likely, Ms. Avila is being protective and just needs some clarification. Perhaps she needs to save face in front of her niece. It could be my sturdy relationship with Amanda will need to suffer right now to protect a more fragile relationship elsewhere.

I can't push this upcoming meeting out of my mind, even though most of the time, the parents I work with are reasonable and supportive. I meet dozens of parents every year who go above and beyond to let me know how much they respect me and stand behind me. They are my champions and heroes. Without them, I would have left the classroom a long time ago. They are parents who truly become partners in their child's educational experience.

Unfortunately, it only takes one or two parents a year to create horrid, anxiety-inducing memories that push their way to the front of my mind whenever upset parents cross my path. When I started teaching, I naively expected parents to support the decisions I made in the classroom. It was shocking to receive that first spiteful and accusatory phone call from a parent who perceives their child has been singled out or treated unjustly. Even worse are the parents who believe the rules don't apply to them or to their children, and that somehow, I have committed the ultimate faux pas by insisting they do.

Over the years, I've developed my own systems for dealing with negative parent interactions—the most effective of which involves putting my response on hold for 24 hours to give me a chance to cool down and gain some perspective. My "24-hour" rule forces me to become more reflective, gather the facts, and respond to upset parents in a way that helps diffuse, rather than further ignite, heated emotions and hurt feelings. Maybe the anxiety building in me as I contemplate the meeting with Ms. Avila stems from not having the usual 24 hours to mentally prepare. I haven't had time to mull over Ms. Avila's hostility, or find some balance and perspective before I head to this meeting. And with five classes still in front of me, I won't have any more time today to think about it. My students need me here, not held hostage by my churning emotions. I cage my anxiety and shove it behind the more pressing and immediate demands of today.

------- ------- -------

I am not late.

I sprint down the stairs to the first-floor conference room and sit down seconds before Ms. Avila enters the room. She has just come from her job as a paralegal at a local law firm. She looks young, but professional. Stable. Confident. I relax a little.

This is going to go well.

Everyone is assembled. Doug begins the introductions, and like a masterful conductor, he guides the conversation to our ultimate purpose. He works slowly and convincingly. My role in today's drama is to sit quietly, speak only when spoken to, and present facts, not emotions. Doug sets the tone by explaining the purpose of the meeting. He carefully reviews his phone conversation with Ms. Avila. He presents the red folder. He allows her to vent her frustrations and reiterate her beliefs: there was no wrongdoing here. We are mistaken.

Her belittling words cut jagged wounds, as intended. It's unsettling to witness her unwavering statements that disavow reality. Her demeanor is still hostile, which doesn't match her image as a mature professional.

It's my turn to talk. I explain the assignment and provide the written directions and scoring rubric. Instead of adding clarity, my presentation results in more agitation. Ms. Avila steps up her assault despite the overwhelming evidence that should have ended this meeting 10 minutes ago.

Doug's patient and warm tone changes. His face flickers with irritation and I can sense Ms. Avila's insistent denials are beginning to grate on him. He changes tactics and grabs a student handbook that contains our code of conduct.

"Ms. Avila, on page 22 of our student handbook, plagiarism is clearly defined, as are the consequences for academic dishonesty. Would you please read this section out loud?"

She reads the first few words, and then hesitates. "I know what it means to plagiarize," she states firmly. "I don't need to read this. I work for a law firm, remember?" She slams the handbook shut on the desk.

Doug cuts her off.

"Ms. Avila, in light of all the evidence presented here today, and in the absence of any other explanation, I must conclude that Amanda did in fact copy her research paper. The evidence of plagiarism is very clear."

Doug scoops the damning papers back into the red folder and closes it forcefully. The end is near, and I wait for the conductor to drop his hands at his side, signaling the end of today's score.

Ms. Avila must have sensed this finality, too. In a final, desperate attempt to prove her point she blurts out, "I know my niece did not cheat. She would never do such a thing. I know she didn't cheat because I wrote the paper for her."

Doug stands up. His hands are quietly at his side.

"This meeting is over."

Exit principal. Exit all.

Day 54

Do you think grades in middle school are important? Why or why not?

"I think grades are important because they show our academic progress and standing, they teach us to be more responsible, and they hold us accountable for our work and effort."
Kaitlyn

"The grade itself essentially doesn't matter but working hard and getting the best you can is important to strive and start off well in high school."
Cali

"Grades don't matter because you can be the smartest in the world but not able to apply knowledge."
Ethan

"Without the grades we wouldn't care. Even if the grades don't go to high school, they still help teach us how to strive for accuracy."
Cooper

Conferences begin today at 11:30 a.m. I need to get moving.

I double check to make sure I have everything I'll need before I head to the gym: water, throat lozenges, snacks, computer, class rosters, extra copies of assignments, class syllabi. What am I forgetting? I'm sure there is something I'll wish I had remembered once I settle in for the first 5-hour session. Ah–pencils. Grab pencils. And pens. Cellphone, just in case I need to check in at home. I doubt I will have time for much texting until my dinner break at 4:30 p.m.

I survey the gym. There are already sets of chairs stacked four deep in front of a small desk I will call home for the next seven and a half hours. A small hourglass timer sits on my desk to help me mark off 5-minute increments, as well as a single, complementary bottle of water. A big banner taped to the gym wall above my desk announces "Chamberlain," in case anyone can't find me in the alphabet soup of teachers whose desks obscure every inch of wall space around the room. I enjoy conferences, even though I will be completely exhausted by the time I head home at 7:30 p.m. Thank goodness tomorrow is a half day, and then it's Thanksgiving break. Surviving conferences in one piece will give me a lot to be thankful for.

I am ready for the onslaught of parents who will swarm the gym as soon as the double doors open. I am ready to reassure, support, and engage. Parents who come to conferences do so with the best intentions and versions of themselves. I glance toward the double doors and notice an occasional head gophering inside, disappearing just as quickly back into the hallway.

The empty chairs in front of me soon fill, and I take inventory of my customers. Brian is here with his parents–working professionals who are still dressed for the office. I see Kayla in the distance and assume there is a parent attached somewhere... Oh, there she is: a large woman with the same blond hair. She towers above the crowd, her body cutting a wide swath as she moves toward my desk. I marvel at the disparity between the two–Kayla is such a tiny, waif-like creature–but the resemblance to her mother was unmistakable. As her mother plows ahead, I hear yelling. "Keep up with me!" the voice insists. "Why are you so slow?" I can easily hear her, even over the commotion. Her unpleasant barbs hit their mark and then suddenly stop. Maybe she realizes she is in public. Kayla's head is bowed as she follows close. I am trapped behind my desk waiting for their arrival and can't intervene right now. Later. Not today. Better not to make a scene. I put on my best smile.

I scan the room for Izzie, but no luck so far. I think she lives with her father, and the chance of them showing up today is slim. Jetmir escorts his mother to a chair near the back of my line and stands next to her, holding a younger sibling who is two or three. We make eye contact, and he smiles and waves. There are swarms of faces I don't recognize overflowing the back of my line. Amanda and her aunt are across the gym, in line to visit another teacher. I doubt they will make it my way today, but it would be good if I could share some kind words–maybe set things on a new path. More faces I recognize fill the seats in front of me until there are no more open spaces. My friend Caroline is there with her daughter, Natalie. McKay's father arrives, still in uniform. He stands up behind the group so another parent can take his chair. Their faces beam with broad smiles, and I feel their warmth; their radiance fills the area in front of my desk like the glow of a campfire.

There is an announcement on the loudspeaker that cuts through the ambient noises:

"Hello, and welcome to fall conferences. We will begin in just a few minutes. Please pick up your child's conference portfolio from the information desk near the double doors where you entered. Please bring this portfolio with you as you visit your child's teachers. Conferences will be limited to five minutes per teacher to ensure everyone has a chance to meet your child's teachers. Thank you and have a great time today!"

I ready my hourglass timer. In most cases, five minutes per student is not nearly enough time. On occasion, it can feel like an eternity.

I motion to Brian's family to come sit in the chairs right in front of my desk.

They smile. I relax a bit. This is a good omen–a good way to start my parent-a-thon. Brian's father loosens his jacket–a beautiful grey houndstooth with a blue silk lining–as he sits. The accents on his tie perfectly match the color of the lining. His trim frame is perfectly polished. Brian's mother is equally well-coifed.

"Thank you for coming to conferences," I begin. "It's so nice to see you. We met at Open House in September, right?"

"Oh yes," Brian's father replies with a confident, booming voice. "We enjoy getting around and meeting all of Brian's teachers." His mother smiles and nods.

"So, tell us," he leans toward me and the mood becomes more intense. "How IS Brian doing in honors science this year?" He glances at the class schedule in his hand. "Fourth period, correct?"

His voice is too loud, like a commercial that startles with its auditory assault in the middle of a TV show.

I pause for a moment before replying. Brian is a stellar student and mature beyond his years. I assume they know exactly how well their son is doing but need some degree of reassurance that he hasn't suddenly and unexpectedly abandoned his superstar habits. I make a split-second decision to let Brian take the lead.

"Brian, how do you think science class is going for you?"

He leans forward in his chair, a little startled but now engaged in our conversation.

"Oh, um," he starts. "How do I think I'm doing? Well... pretty good, I'd say. It's been a good quarter. Yeah, good."

He pauses and looks at me, not quite sure where to go next. He is unusually quiet and small; not at all like the young man I've witnessed in class these past weeks.

"Have you had a chance to show your parents your portfolio?" I ask.

He remembers the portfolio in his lap and opens it up on the desk. I lean in toward Brian's father, mimicking his body language. His mother continues to shrink into the background of our conversation.

"Here are some examples that show Brian's dedication to excellence. His work is quite impressive, and it reveals his strong analytical skills," I add.

His father surveys the portfolio, thoughtfully turning pages.

"Well, as you know, Brian is an honors student," he says. "What I really want to know is, can he raise his grade from a 97.4%, which I see is where he's at currently, to a 100%? There is no reason for him to earn less than a perfect score, ever. He knows we expect the best from him."

By now, Brian has receded back into his chair. His mother glances over to me as if to offer a small apology for her husband's smothering intensity. I move as far forward as I can without pushing my desk into Brian's father and match the loud boom of his voice.

"Brian is doing an outstanding job in science class. In fact, his scores are at the very top of the class. While he is always welcome to redo any assignment he chooses, please know his grade represents 10 weeks of excellence. I am very proud of Brian's effort and accomplishments."

Not to mention he is an amazing human being.

This seems to have done the trick. His tone changes and he leans back into his chair, away from me.

"Well, I am glad to hear he is working at the top of the class. That's where he should be."

I glance at the hourglass timer on the desk. The final 15 seconds worth of sand falls, grain by grain, through the tiny opening in the middle. I need several more minutes with this family, but I am not going to get it. The line of parents who are shuffling forward impatiently now extends past my rows of chairs. The gym is full of the sound of chairs scraping on the polished wood floor. There's no way to dole out five more precious minutes on the hourglass without causing a riot. I have no choice but to finish.

"It looks like our time is just about up for today. Are there any other quick questions you'd like to ask?"

Brian's father stands up and buttons his suit jacket. His intense gaze vanishes, and he slaps on a quick smile. He is done for today. I am dismissed.

"No, I think we're done here. Nice to see you again, Mrs. Chamberlain."

As Brian's father turns to leave, his mother quickly presses a gift card discreetly into my hand. Her grip lingers. Her hesitant smile becomes more confident as the distance between husband and wife widens.

"Brian loves your class," she offers. "Thank you for everything you are doing for him. I know he is very excited to start his STEM project." In an instant, she releases my hand and turns to leave.

I have mere moments to reflect on the inner workings of this family—the complexity of their interactions—before the next group plops down in the chairs in front of me. I flip the hourglass. I take a sip of water. One down.

I smile. I welcome. I flip the hourglass again. And again. And again.

Still holding his little brother in his lap, Jetmir translates for his mother. The family emigrated from Albania a few years ago, and her language skills are still emerging. I don't bother calling over one of the district-provided translators to monitor our conversation; I can tell from her expression that Jetmir is a trustworthy communicator. Jetmir has already determined the topic for his STEM project, and we spend most of our meager conference time excitedly discussing his idea: a device for monitoring sunspot activity. The design is simple and elegant. The uniqueness of his idea surprises me, and I can tell from his mother's excited replies that she is proud of her son. I feel proud, too, even though he's only been my student for a few weeks. My contributions to his success have been minimal at this point. I let myself enjoy this moment, even if I didn't completely earn it.

The line of waiting parents should be dwindling by now, but it isn't. My legs are stiff from sitting in one position for so long, so I shift in my seat and stretch out my legs under the desk. My voice feels fatigued and water no longer soothes its raspiness, so I switch to lozenges. I have another hour to go before our half-hour dinner break.

More welcomes and smiles. Tired faces. Hesitant questions. Furrowed brows. A few more surreptitiously offered gift cards.

No sign yet of Izzie or her family. If they don't make it to conferences, I must find some other way to get in touch with them and open a line of communication. Maybe I'll try my postcard trick.

For now, I hold out hope.

December: Days 60-74

The Importance of Breaks

Though I've always enjoyed school, the amount of work can often be overwhelming, especially when added to the other activities I participate in outside of the school day. One of the most important pieces for cultivating learning is to allow breaks so you can recharge mentally. Finding some time to decompress is as much an instrumental part of success as working hard and challenging yourself.

Amelia D., 15

Day 66

The classroom is quiet and uncharacteristically devoid of its usual chatter.

The quiet envelops the class like a layer of fog that sweeps in from the ocean on a lazy July afternoon, cooling the warm summer air and layering mystery over the sparkling sand.

My 4th period students are deep into their STEM research papers on engineering and science topics they have selected. Tomorrow is the last day to work in class. After that, they will finish their drafts at home and present them for peer editing next Monday. Final versions are due next Friday, the day before winter break.

I am not sure which I prefer—the quiet or the chatter—but today I need a little break.

I didn't have my usual planning period today. I spent it downstairs working with Micah. He's serving a three-day in-school suspension. I don't know what happened to land him there, and I don't really want to; I am just relieved that it didn't happen in 5th period.

The in-school suspension room is narrow and stuffy and uninviting; it's a room without windows or fresh air, the kind of place that makes my claustrophobia kick in. I work for as long as I can, fighting the urge to bolt. Micah and I are using his musings and ideas to create a paragraph outline, complete with topic sentences. As difficult as he can be in a group, I enjoy working with him one-on-one. He is funny. And charming. And as I am discovering, he is also smart. He cannot focus, but I know it is not his fault. He tries to follow along as I patiently explain the directions, but even when it is just the two of us, it is hard to keep him on track. I wonder how much he'll be able to finish today on his own. He struggles to translate his thoughts to text, and most of the time his writing is unintelligible. I create a sticky to remind myself to check in at the end of the day. My next two mornings will be spent working with him, but I write another note to check on library space. Maybe we can at least find a cheerier workspace.

I give my classroom a quick glance. Jay, Aden, and Clarissa are sitting three abreast at their table designed for two. Their gangly pubescent arms and legs knock into each other while they work, heads bent. Natalie pulls up a chair on the opposite side of the table and sits side-straddle, balancing her laptop on her knees. Desks and chairs have been rearranged in stark contrast to my usual orderly design, but it doesn't matter. They are working hard. I don't dare move or speak, for fear of disrupting their silence. My usual sashaying around the classroom and cheerful commentary will have to wait for another time.

What I really want to do right now is snoop in our shared files and read their works in progress and offer some kudos, or maybe even some edits. But it seems wrong to charge in uninvited, like a houseguest who peruses your medicine cabinets. Trust is an important aspect of our relationship. I can't just barge in and start offering suggestions without at least causing some irritation, or at worst, creating hurt feelings or forcing my students into shut-down mode. It's one thing to warn students I will be opening their files or offering editing, but it's another issue completely to violate their space and offer feedback too soon. I wish I had planned today a little more thoroughly. Maybe I wouldn't be sitting here with a dead-quiet class and 48 precious minutes of class time remaining.

Suddenly, sticky notes seem like a good idea. Still in stealth mode, I inventory my supplies. I have plenty of yellow and green. Okay. What if I use them as a kind of code—a way for my students to let me know if they are ready for some warm feedback or edits? My projector is already on, so I open a new document and type this up on the screen:

I can see you are working diligently on your research papers.

If you are interested in having me read your paper and offer some warm feedback, take a yellow sticky note and put it on the top corner of your screen.

If you'd like some warm feedback plus editing suggestions, use a green sticky note instead.

No sticky note? I won't be reading your paper today. Maybe tomorrow—but not today.

Let me know how I can help you.

As I am typing, a few students look up from their screens. The broken rhythm causes a momentary shift of focus. Message received. I set the sticky notes out on an extra desk, go back to my computer, and wait.

And wait some more.

Huh. Maybe they didn't see the sticky notes. I move them to the front counter where I know everyone can see them.

It's hard to be patient. At this point in the school year, they should know they can trust me—to be kind, to be fair, to be honest. Maybe too honest. Maybe what they need right now is less honesty and more encouragement. As the minutes tick by, the class is eerily quiet. I am starting to second-guess my approach. Should I have simply opened their research documents and read them anyway? Left thoughtful notes in the comments section? It doesn't matter. I won't go back on my word.

Heads are bent. They are working furiously and, right now, they don't need me.

The tiny analog clock on my desk silently displays every second and minute of my failure. The secondhand bears witness to my self-inflicted predicament and for a moment, it appears to point in my direction through its glass cover, proffering a crooked finger to scold me like a character out of a Dickens novel. Warning me. "Don't do it–don't open their documents. You promised."

The little bitch.

I feel properly chastised.

Fuck that damn clock.

The sticky notes are gathering dust on my front table and I am now stuck with keeping my promise. Clearly, this class needs their space. I am trying not to feel hurt that no one will allow me a peek at their work. Their secrecy surprises me and stings a little.

I see a hand go up–hey, LOOK! A hand just went up! –so I pop out of my seat and approach Brian quietly. He needs me! Finally, someone needs me. I knew if I waited patiently and calmly that they would start to ask for help.

"Hey–how can I help you, Brian?" It feels good to be needed. I holster some of my enthusiasm.

"Uhm, can I go to the bathroom, Mrs. C?"

WTF? You called me over here to ask if you could use the bathroom? Are you serious?

"Yes...yes, of course," I answer softly. "Just sign out in the back of the room."

They really don't need me. At least, not today.

No feeling sorry for myself.

You offered. They accepted. End of story.

Day 74

t's Friday.

I feel like I've been holding my breath for a week, and my lungs are ready to explode.

It is 2:19 p.m., and we have arrived at the final class of the longest week in teaching: the week before winter break. The classroom hums with anticipation and impatience. My students chat excitedly and wait anxiously by their chairs, though a few slowly inch closer to the exit door, hoping I don't notice. They wait to hurtle into the hallways toward their temporary freedom. In the final few seconds together, I ask them about their holiday plans. Some of them even ask me about mine. I smile. Even I feel impatient, irritated this is taking so long.

Just let them out the damn door.

The week before winter break is a nearly indomitable challenge, even for veteran teachers. There is no way to describe the enormous amount of preparation that has gone into making this week a success. Only years of practice can teach one how to navigate this emotional time of year.

Perhaps the most important lesson I've learned: This break means different things for different students. For some students, the time off means elaborate trips and enriching experiences. Earlier in the week they approach me, form in hand, informing me their vacation will be starting early. They need both my signature, and any work they might miss due to their early departure (because of course they will take time to complete it while on a cruise ship or in line for the ski lift). They share their plans, giddy with excitement. I feel happy for them and know their adventures will be a much needed and enlightening break from school.

For other students, winter break is a time of uncertainty and instability. They know it. I know it. School represents stability. Warmth. Acceptance. Food. Emotional support. There is a firm dividing line in my school (and in most schools) between the "haves" and the "have-nots" of students. I teach in a relatively affluent district where about 25% of our student body qualifies for "free and reduced" lunch–a marker of poverty defined by the federal government. To put the numbers into perspective: I teach about 116 students each school day, spread over five class periods. Students in my Environmental Science class, like Izzie and

Camden, I see twice—once in Environmental Science, and later in their regular 8th grade science class. Statistically, about 29 of these students are living at or below the poverty level.

For me, these are not just numbers. They are faces, full of hope. They are students, full of intelligence and potential. They are open, impressionable young hearts.

There is only so much I can do to help prepare them for the next two weeks. A coat here. Warm clothes there. Reassurances all around. Some of these students receive extra bags of food on Fridays to sustain them over the weekends. I am sure they are wondering what will happen over break without that bag of food on Friday—I know I am. I know some of these students will move over break, and I won't see them again. Every year, I must reconcile my emotions: excitement, for some… grief, for others.

The bell rings and in record time, my classroom empties—almost. Amanda holds back long enough to tell me she will miss me. I tell her I will miss her too, and it's true. Her hesitation to leave catches me off-guard. Maybe this signals a new beginning—a chance to begin repairing our fractured relationship.

I exhale a sigh of relief when my classroom has cleared. I feel a small twinge of guilt for being happy to see them go, but I'm also sad it will be two weeks before we reunite.

I wave to students in the hallway. There are hoots and hollers and the occasional high-five, until finally the last student exits. The hallway is quiet. I am free now, too.

Before I can leave, I need to make sure I am ready for my first day back. Over the years I've learned I need the peace of mind that comes with setting myself up for a strong return. I quickly prep my lesson plans for the first day back, print a few documents that I will need, and do one final walk-through. The process reminds me of a military inspection—perhaps my Army background coming through.

I've decided against bringing homework to correct over the break. There is a small voice that tells me I could get ahead of the game if I just took a few hours here and there, but the rest of my mind is too exhausted to take this advice. Papers will have to wait until the new year.

Right now, "next year" seems far in the distance, comfortably out of view.

I am not sure who needs this break more—them, or me.

January: Days 76-90

Rocky Roads

Hey Mrs. Chamberlain,

So, I'm sure by now you have probably heard that I stapled my hand today in class and had to go to the ER to get it removed. Laughing is allowed. I am sure you are probably thinking to yourself "this kid is an idiot" but with stronger words. I have learned my lesson about listening to adults and NOT STAPLING THINGS TO MYSELF, but I understand that there will be consequences.

Also—can I get my homework for tonight? That would be great.

Have a great night and sorry for stapling my hand.

Mason M., 14

Day 75-almost

I f January had a motto, it would probably be something like, "Expect the unexpected," or "Predict the unpredictable."

Happy New Year.

It's back-to-school tomorrow, and I am panicking.

It is 5:15 a.m.–my usual wake-up time–but this morning, something is different. Even before I move a muscle to sit up, I can feel my heart racing–loud thuds echoing in my eardrums. I consider potential culprits: New Year Eve post-celebration regret? Not likely considering my alcohol was limited to one glass of wine over a rousing game of Apples to Apples. Caffeine? Okay, no–I'm still in bed. No coffee yet. After eliminating a few more explanations, I realize I am having a good old-fashioned panic attack.

There is only one culprit: knowing no matter how prepared I am to return to work tomorrow, this month will feel like driving down a pothole-filled country road at full speed, trying to anticipate the next bump. January is like starting the school year all over again. Despite years of experience in the driver's seat, I know I will miss only a handful of those potholes, but squarely hit others. I know at times I will have to choose one in order to avoid another, and I hope my past excursions will guide me in the right direction. The best thing I can do during this bumpy ride is make sure I have my seatbelt securely fastened.

I reluctantly log in to my school account for the first time in two weeks and spend the rest of the morning answering emails like this one: "Mrs. Chamberlain, I am sorry to bother you during break but I am wondering why [X] assignment is listed as missing in the grade book and can I get a copy of it?" I've been adding meeting requests to my calendar, outlining lessons for the month, and contacting my teaching partner, Heather, to finalize tomorrow's plans–a new engineering challenge we wrote together that incorporates popsicle sticks and play dough.

She is at school today—our last day of vacation—working. She just offered to organize all our supplies for tomorrow. She is a saint.

I feel bad she is there, and I am not. I text her back with a promise of coffee in the morning, and this assuages my guilt somewhat for now.

January has arrived. Buckle up, baby.

Day 77

Yesterday I was absent from class. It was not my choice. I was assigned to attend a training two days after our return from the holiday break.

It sucked for me... but it sucked worse for my substitute teacher.

Working as a substitute teacher is the hardest job I've ever had.

And that is saying a lot.

Before I became a teacher, I had some crazy-ass jobs. I went into the military right out of high school, and after my training, I was sent to a tactical unit in Frankfurt, Germany. We would roll our tanks and tracked vehicles out to the field and set up shop for two or three weeks at a time, working 12-hour shifts intercepting Russian radio transmissions in the 1980s–near the end of the Cold War. After I completed my four-year stint, I got an on-campus job at the university I was attending and ended up overseeing the media center for months, because my boss quit with no replacement. Between classes, I would rush over to the media center to check on client orders and supervise my colleagues. It was too much responsibility, and not enough pay. I worked one summer pouring ceramic doll heads, experienced the agony of minimum-wage work in a fabric store, and waitressed. I've been a stay-at-home mom, home-business worker, and headhunter, recruiting engineers to work for companies like Lockheed Martin and Bally's Gaming. I once had a job handing accounts payable and receivable for a small home security company, a position for which I could not have been less qualified. During the interview, my future boss–who was high on cocaine at the time–amused himself by asking me to say something in Russian. I cheerfully gave him my favorite vulgarity, which literally means "fuck your mother." When he asked what I had said, I told him, "glad to meet you".

Like I said: I've had some strange, awkward, and downright-awful jobs.

But none of these experiences prepared me for substitute teaching. Showing up as a substitute is like walking into a room where cleverly hidden incendiary devices will explode randomly and without provocation throughout the day. You can try to prepare yourself, read the sub plans, (if the teacher was thoughtful enough to leave any), memorize names and seating charts, bring extra activities, be prepared to play games or watch movies... but no amount of preparation will protect you from the explosions that destroy any learning opportunities you may have been attempting to create.

With middle school students, your success or failure is directly related to the strength of your relationship with each student; as a substitute, you have no relationships to rely on. You are doomed.

At some point in the day–boom.

You might survive until 6th period. But that last class of the day? It's going to be a killer.

Teachers know this. Substitutes know this. Thank God they keep coming back to our rooms. Teaching happens 180 days per year, whether we are in the classroom or not. We don't have the luxury of cancelling classes when we are vomiting at 5 a.m. or assigned to attend a training or conference in the middle of a school week. We don't take vacation or purposely plan outside appointments once the school year has begun. Most teachers I know make every effort to be at school–often at the expense of their families, their health, and their sanity. In this system, we accumulate weeks and weeks of sick days, all-too aware of the chaos created by our absence.

At the beginning of each school year, most teachers (but not all) spend an inordinate amount of time carefully creating folders for our future substitute teachers that contain seating charts, health updates, daily schedules, phone lists, extra lesson plans, passwords–you name it. Everything we can think of that might make a substitute teacher's day a little easier to navigate goes in these folders. It is not a detonation-proof system, but it helps.

Returning to school after a sub day means dealing with all the shit that jumped off while you were out: rowdy students, unfinished assignments, poorly executed lessons that need to be retaught, discipline referrals, missed meetings… And then there are the obscure, inexplicable events that transcend all logic–but then, there is nothing logical about middle schoolers. The prefrontal cortex, which oversees decision-making processes, is rendered useless by the onset of puberty hormones. I had a student once who successfully hid inside one of my large storage cabinets under a lab table. He went undetected for hours, playing games on his Chromebook. He was finally discovered because he was banging around and making too much noise. When I asked him later why he did such a damn fool thing, he told me it was because he missed me. Sometimes, kids feel abandoned when their teachers leave. They don't realize it, but their misbehavior is a way to punish us for being gone–or at least regain our attention when we return.

Sometimes, kids just act like fools.

And Mason? Well, he is not the student I would have predicted would get in trouble. But again, this is January.

I read his email when I arrived at school the morning after my training. He had asked a friend to help him staple the soft part of his hand between his thumb and first finger because he felt bored. His body had an allergic reaction to the metal in the staple, and he ended up at the emergency room for four hours to get it removed. On top of this, his incredible parents had the wherewithal to require him to write me a letter of apology after he returned home. I figure he's had enough consequences.

Sometimes experience really is the best teacher.

February: Days 91-110

The Do-Over

A good teacher will teach the subject, get their students to pass the class, but not much more.

A great teacher will influence their students to both excel in the class, but also to pursue the subject further, conduct research, and inspire them to look at the subject and the class as more than just a grade.

Michael S., 14

Day 100

Today is the 100th day of the school year.

It is a chilly morning, even for February in the Pacific Northwest. It snowed three days ago and, though the roads were plowed, and painstakingly sanded, smog-encrusted remnants of winter's wrath remain piled on the side streets and parking lots. The heavy, chilly air has yet to dissipate and I sense its weight. I am going to leave a little early this morning to drive the 10 miles to school; this includes going up a steep state highway infamous for one of the worst accident records in the state. I am not looking forward to the drive.

Coincidentally, today is also Valentine's Day.

I love Valentine's Day. When I was growing up, I had a great-aunt who celebrated the holiday each year by sending me a card and $20 bill. My family moved a great deal while I was growing up, but she seemed to find me regardless. I remember the years when I was stationed in Frankfurt, living off a specialist's salary and renting a small apartment on the economy in downtown Hoechst. The sudden appearance of her card meant an evening out and dinner—an unexpected pleasure at such a meager time in my life. I still cherish memories of walks in the crisp evening air near the river Main. Holding hands. Shivers—not from the cold, but from kisses on the back of my neck. Lovely memories. I think she made me fall in love with the idea of this day and its symbolic celebration of the heart.

I don't want to go to work today. For one day, I wish I could make up some ridiculous excuse not to be there. A rapid-onset illness or forgotten dentist appointment would be helpful right now. Maybe a fun little 24-hour stomach bug. That would work. Nothing too severe or extreme—just enough to reshape my reality for one day. I would like to play hooky. Cut out little hearts from thick red and pink construction paper and create a card for my someone special. Take a hot bath after a long walk. Indulge in an afternoon nap. I would like a selfish middle-of-the-week day.

I just...can't.

Duty nags at my subconscious. Even taking the time to create marginal plans for a substitute would take 20 or 30 minutes. I need an hour to do a respectable job; a substitute's job in middle school is too hard to justify leaving shitty, half-baked plans for the day–especially on Valentine's Day. Bound to my lofty ideologies, I bundle up and grab my boots. Today is a boot day, for sure.

Day 100. That means no more excuses. I am over halfway through the school year, with midterms in the rear view. My students' results hold me accountable for their success or failure to this point. I've been poring over the results for the past few days and have found mixed outcomes. Some of my students are showing clear gains; others are not. When I compare their results to their September pre-tests, I can't help but feel I have not done enough.

It will never be enough. Not for me, not for the public, and not for my 116 kids.

The 116 represent every cross section of the student body: gifted students and students with learning disabilities in equal proportion, athletes, members of the student council. The homeless and disenfranchised. Students with burgeoning drug problems and legal challenges. The wealthy and entitled. Students who believe they can be successful in school, and young teenagers who have already lost hope for their future. Science is a required class for all students, period. Their presence in my classroom isn't up to them–or me.

I teach them all.

I welcome them all.

I create a space for them all.

There is never enough time for them all.

They do not arrive at my doorstep with equal skill sets. In August, when I first had access to my class lists, I began reviewing test data from previous school years in order to create a profile of each class. Each class profile is unique and reveals both skills and learning deficits. This year, all the students in my 5th period class are reading at a 4th grade level or below. Not a single student in that class can read at grade level; yet, here they are in 8th grade science, where the expectation is that they will somehow, miraculously, learn 8th grade science content. The public expects all students will succeed and produce equal (not equitable) results by the end of their 180 days with me, regardless of the students' individual starting points. It is my job to foster a classroom environment that allows students to learn and blossom and engage. I am reminded that if I am a skilled, caring, and engaging teacher, I can lessen the divide between the "haves" and the "have-nots." The well-intentioned system which holds me accountable for student test scores in turn refuses to acknowledge the inherent inequalities our students face, or the role these play in future outcomes.

I've been taught throughout my career that teachers are the single greatest factor to influence the success or failure of our students. Maybe it's true.

Sometimes though, I wonder.

While I drive towards school, I mull over their progress. Based on their midterms, I can predict–with relative accuracy based on my years of experience–who will pass the upcoming state assessments and who will not.

Jetmir will pass. His scores are solid. Though English is his second language, his strong analytical skills are evident. He makes clear connections between data and result. He provides thoughtful reflection. He is on track for the success we have defined for him.

Kayla and Izzie are in danger of failing. Micah, too. While I can cite many exemplars of accomplishment this year–students who overcome the odds against them–I fixate on those I have yet to help. I don't know if I can make a difference for them. Izzie is out this week on another suspension. I think it was for fighting. It's her third offense this year. I tried to call her home (again), but the number we have for her family has been disconnected. I won't be able to talk with her father. At this point, there is no chance for her to stay caught up in either science class. She has an older sister in high school; I will call the head secretary after school today and see if they have any new contact information. I am getting desperate. My next step will be to get her cell number from friends. Without some way of communicating, I feel helpless. I would drive to her home, but I heard she and her father had moved again. I worry I am on the brink of losing her forever. Ira asked about her on Tuesday, noting her absence. I know he is concerned, too.

Micah is off his meds and, at this rate, won't make it through the school year. His attendance is spotty at best. By the time he gets to science class he is wound up; his distractibility makes it impossible to learn. The whole class is suffering as a result of his presence. The solution to Micah's problem seems simple, but without cooperation from his parents there is nothing I can do. I can remove him from the room when he is completely out of control, but it is a temporary fix. My 5th period class is in free-fall.

Their success or failure rests squarely on my shoulders.

By the time I pull into the parking lot, I feel the weight of blame.

Day 103

"**W**here are the extra glue sticks?"

"What?"

"Glue? Where is the extra glue, Mrs. C?"

I shout across the room. "Look in the drawer underneath my guitar. There might be another box in there." My guitar is hanging behind my desk.

"What?"

Gabby can't hear me. I am all the way across the room, buried under a pile of construction paper and display boards. My stomach growls. The pizza isn't here yet. Damn it. I ordered it an hour ago. Isn't there some sort of delivery guarantee, like "60 minutes or it's free"?! Right now, I can't remember the name of the company where I ordered the pizza. The number is still on my phone under Recent. I could call them, but it takes too much effort. I am so tired. And it is so loud in here. Mind-numbingly loud. I can't think.

I motion downwards and she sees me. Her head disappears behind my desk.

I can barely breathe.

My classroom is at crowd capacity and spilling over into Heather's room, which is quieter. I feel a twinge of jealousy as I try to wade through the excitement and pandemonium in my own room. I am sure there is a sign somewhere on the wall indicating maximum occupancy—which we have surely exceeded. Heather is next door cutting out titles for the display boards from her Criqut. These damned trifold boards are so time consuming and unnecessary. Our students had created thoughtful digital presentations using Google Slides for our school fair, and even created short videos of their experimental trials that are embedded in their slides. But, of course, we can't use them in subsequent competitions.

It's depressing how entrenched science fairs are in paper-based displays. So last year. So out-of-touch with the technological world that permeates every facet of their lives. Last year we brought (well, snuck) our Chromebooks to the district competition and showed the videos to the judges. It wasn't allowed, per se, but the judges loved the innovative approach. This year, we've been asked to bring the videos again—a small win. I cringe every year around this time reading the memes and jokes on social media about parents' disdain for science fairs and all the related preparations. It is not a surprise to me that our country ranks far behind other first-world nations in science.

Two words: Display. Boards.

Despite the escalating decibels, I occasionally hear Heather's voice as she discusses title options with each student. I admire her calmness. We've both been at school since before 6:30 a.m. preparing for this final night before tomorrow's district science fair. She has more patience than I do after a long day of teaching—or at least, she always seems patient.

Heather loves all things geology. Her science passions and interests are the opposite of mine, which has helped create such a symbiotic relationship between us. Our combined strengths bring a wealth of wisdom to the students. Each year she teaches half the 8th graders, and I get the other half. Occasionally we swap students if we end up with a bad mix in a class. It's amazing how just changing one or two students can alter the psychology of an entire group. I hate giving up my students, though—even the tough ones. I know Heather feels the same way.

Sky and Josh are already here, and their board is covered with fake blood to imitate a blood splatter pattern. Their forensic science investigation already medaled in our school fair. Victoria is working on her social sciences project about the relationship between moon phases and human behavior. Camden and Mattias are crunching data, and they have layered their graphs and charts on their board neatly in flip-chart fashion. I've never seen two students with the ability to analyze data the way they have. I suspect they will qualify for the state competition. Their project about the impact of breakfast on learning is simple; yet they've managed to take a relatively straightforward concept and create brilliance. That is the true art of this competition: take a simple idea and make it your own. We have 23 8th graders moving on to districts this year. If they present well tomorrow, they will advance to state. It is a banner year.

I see Kayla in the corner quietly placing her title in position, getting ready to glue each piece in place. She works slowly and methodically. She isn't part of the chatter and hum—she is in a bubble all by herself. Maybe I should go over and check on her? It is a long walk from one side of the classroom to the other, with multiple stops along the way to offer help or reassurances. It will take me a good 10 minutes to get over there. She is not actually alone; Brian has moved his board closer to hers. They aren't talking, exactly, but his presence seems to fill the void she has created around her.

The arriving pizza elicits cheers and hoots from both rooms. The noise is deafening but the smell of hot, sticky cheese and tomato sauce snaps me to attention. Jetmir and Cooper move into the classroom, their arms piled with boxes. A few wrestlers linger at the door, offering to help us eat the pizza. I hate having to send them off–I am sure they are hungry–but there isn't enough pizza for a dozen or so hungry teenage wrestlers. I know they understand, but I feel guilty.

"Salam, Mrs. C!" I hear Jetmir's voice from behind the pile. "Where do you want these?"

I can't help but laugh, despite the hour and my tiredness. He just finished a two-hour practice for his upcoming wrestling championships; and yet, he is still cheerful and energetic. Like Josh and Sky, he medaled at our school fair with a sunspot detector. He is such an enthusiastic member of this team. He's a natural leader: kind and thoughtful, never too busy to help someone else. An old soul, really. I know I need to find some energy–readjust my attitude to sustain me through the rest of this evening and the long weekend ahead. This time of year is a marathon of competitions, one right after another, both exhausting and exhilarating. State finals are at the end of March, and we might even have a few students selected to compete at nationals. It seems like the craziness will never end–right up until it does.

I take a cue from Jetmir and add some cheer and kindness to my voice.

It's a good start.

I keep hoping Izzie will show up, but I already know she won't. She can't. She was suspended yesterday for fighting. Again. This is her 3rd–no, maybe 4th–time. She is out of this competition cycle. Students must work their way up the ladder; one event leads to the next. If she misses tomorrow, she won't be able to go to state. Her work with Ira has been incredible: a project about DDT residue in oceans, and how it affects the neurology of barnacles. Ira found a lab that would test her water samples for free. The two of them have been working together on Tuesdays–every spare moment, their heads are back in the prep room testing filter configurations and measuring water into tiny beakers. I wish I could find a competition path for her, but at this point it might be too late. I don't know. I need to do some research.

She's worked too hard–we've all worked too hard–to let her suspension derail an entire year's worth of work.

There must be a way.

March: Days 111-131

Perseverance

Middle school is what you make of it. Work hard. Be present in the world. Pay attention and get the most out of things. My family is split, meaning I live with my mother in one house, and my father in another, which causes problems in itself. On top of that, I am a student and an athlete. Putting all of that together, I face difficulties–and they sometimes get out of hand. In these moments, it's easy to put my head down and let my problems overflow. But those difficulties can be avoided. You have the choice of which road you want to turn on.

    Aden D., 14

To: All Staff
From: Doug
Re: Emergency Staff Meeting

Good Morning Monarchs,

Today after school at 3:30 p.m. there will be a brief (15 minute) staff meeting. I apologize for the late notice, but I have important information I need to share with the whole staff. Please plan on arriving on time so I can finish quickly.
Have a great Monarch Day!

Doug
Principal

Day 111

run into Dan.

I literally run right into him.

Bang.

He is holding the library door open for me, smiling. A polite, end-of-the-day, "hang in there, we're nearly finished" kind of smile.

My reckless collision throws me off-kilter; my shoulder grazes the metal door frame and my knee hits the edge, hard. He throws his arm out in front of me the way a parent might protect a child from an opening car door or the sharp edge of a coffee table.

The pain in my knee forces me to look up, and I realize I've inadvertently shoved him into the opposite side of the frame. I feel the blush on my face starting, partly from my throbbing knee, but mostly from the embarrassment of my mindlessness. I can see from his kind eyes that apologies are unnecessary, but I stammer through one regardless.

Dan follows me to a table where Heather has saved us seats. It's only 3:32 p.m., but the remaining tables are already full. How did everyone get here so quickly? My room is right down the hall from the library; in fact, only Heather's room is closer. Maybe they dismissed their classes a little early? It happens. It doesn't matter how, really.

I feel heartened that my colleagues took Doug's request so seriously. By now, my knee really starts to throb, and I lean down to see there is a small gash in my leggings. Damn it. I don't even care about the blood stain, but the leggings will have to be replaced. One more thing to take care of later–after sticky notes and after science fair planning.

Science fair. My mind begins to wander. Oh yes. I need to touch base with Doug after the meeting about transportation for state. A bus. Yes, we are going to need a bus for sure. I still can't believe it–21 students are going. We might be the largest team in state history. Jetmir can't go; he has state wrestling finals the same weekend. Kayla qualified, but dropped out. I am sad about losing them, and not sure why Kayla isn't going. She didn't tell me. I didn't ask.

I'm tired.

Dan gives me a reassuring look from across the table, bringing me back to the here and now.

I lean in toward Heather. "Do you have any idea what this meeting is about?"

She shakes her head. We only have a few seconds to speculate, as Doug is about to make his way to the front of the group. I haven't seen her all day, even though our rooms are next to each other, separated only by a small storage area where we keep all our microscopes, samples, and supplies. Sometimes we prop open the doors to the storage area to give the effect of connecting our rooms. It's fun to comingle our groups during work time. Her classroom usually ends up being the quiet work room, flooded with soft music, minions, and dim lighting. It makes a nice contrast to my 80s rock.

"Thank you everyone for arriving so promptly. I will be brief so we can get you on your way." Doug clears his throat. His eyes scan the room and I watch him make eye contact with each teacher, one after another. His eyes look kind, but serious. I feel a twinge in the pit of my stomach. He hasn't called us here for good news.

My mind races, considering all the possibilities. Terminally ill student? Parent complaint? RIFs? Oh my gosh—that must be it. I bet the district is going to lay off staff this year. There have been rumblings and whispers about funding shortfalls for months. The timing is about perfect for such an announcement. And of course, he wouldn't announce RIFs via email. That would be such an asshole thing to do— and Doug is most definitely not one. No wonder he looks so pained. I am trying to listen to his words as my mind struggles to fathom the ramifications of staff reductions. Heather and I are probably safe. Dan, too. Reductions in force are always considered based on seniority, and we are far enough up the ladder we won't be pink slipped. I scan the room, trying to decide which teachers are most at risk.

Doug continues, "Some of you may know this already, but last year I lost a friend—someone I have known since college. He died unexpectedly of a heart attack at only 56 years old. When you lose someone like that, so suddenly, it changes you. I realized in all the years I knew him; I had never told him that I loved him. I am sure he knew it—but I had never actually said the words."

The room is still. Not even an inhale or exhale punctuates the silence.

"I am sure...well," he pauses for a microsecond, "I hope you know by now how I feel about each and every one of you. But in case you don't, I need to tell you that I love you."

Doug's eyes are red, and I notice for the first time the tell-tale puffiness. He's been crying.

Wow.

He must really be upset about these layoffs.

I've never seen him so emotional. Until this moment, I would have described him as a pragmatic problem solver. Not a crier.

I hear a voice from the back of the room. "We love you too, Doug!" The silence is abruptly broken while a tiny ripple of uncomfortable laughter fills the room. Doug seems frozen in place. A teacher in the front row stands and wraps his arms around Doug in a big bear hug. It's Eric, our Harley Davidson-riding shop teacher. Eric's long bushy beard completely hides Doug's face.

The commotion settles. As Eric moves back through the front row, he hugs everyone in his path. Maybe it's his attempt to relieve some of the obvious tension in the room.

Doug turns resolutely towards us, determined to finish.

Here it comes.

"Effective Friday, I am resigning my position as principal. Please know this was my choice—and I am happy to be moving on to the next phase of my life. I will miss you, but I know you will be in good hands for the remainder of the school year."

I am trying to listen. I can't hear the new principal's name. My ears fill with the rushing sound of my own blood punctuated by a staccato drumming heartbeat. My breath catches on my tongue, its raspy tone adding to the cacophony flooding my brain.

"Jim worked as an assistant principal at the high school, and I know he is well-qualified to lead you forward. This transition was approved in an emergency board meeting last week."

Jim Whatever-his-last-name-is steps forward. He is young and well-groomed. His suit looks new. He shakes Doug's hand and stands awkwardly as the room suddenly explodes in noise.

Bodies crowd around Doug, but the path toward Jim is unobstructed. He is left to bear witness, however uncomfortably, to our unfiltered mourning and outpouring of surprise and grief.

I've read the brain deals with pain in a funny way—blocking or ignoring lesser pain to reveal the more fundamental and overwhelming wounds, or life-threatening incidents that must be treated immediately. Our brains categorize the threat level, prioritizing the new emergency over the previous. Shock is nature's painkiller.

I stand, and the pain in my knee is gone.

People in shock tend toward one of a few primary reactions: fight, flight, or freeze. I command my feet to fly toward an exit sign, or shuffle into a crowded corner and lose myself in the uproar and conversations.

I am frozen in place. My feet will not obey.

The seconds tick by slowly, reverberating in my subconscious. After what seems like an eternity, I force a step in Jim's direction.

I am not being kind or heroic. I am being necessary.

Another step. I see his outstretched hand reaching towards me.

Flight isn't in the cards.

Instead, I stay in the fight.

Day 125

F or two weeks, my Environmental Science class has been researching and creating upcycled products to present at our very first "Shark Tank: Upcycled"– a piece of curriculum I wrote and modeled after the popular TV series. Students can work by themselves or with a partner to create a product made from items you would normally throw away or banish to the corner of a garage or shed: old license plates, broken clocks, shattered baseball bats, discarded horseshoes, plastic containers–the list goes on and on. With our incessant consumption of natural resources and insatiable appetite for consumer goods, it is possible at some point in the not-too-distant future, we will exhaust our global supply of available, virgin resources. Upcycling is becoming a more popular option for creating usable items that have a monetary value.

This might be my favorite project–and the best one I've ever created. Dan helped me add a math component: a spreadsheet that allows students to show cost-versus-profit analysis. Students must conceptualize a product and build a scale model to bring into the Tank, then sell the product to us investors by convincing us of its marketability and potential use. I have been busy recruiting a cast of teachers as members of the Tank. Ira wants to be "Mr. Wonderful." I am sure he will be hilarious as the curmudgeonly investor.

Aden and Cooper have teamed up and are doing something sports related. Gabby is working on some type of plant-feeding system using old plastic bottles. I haven't seen Mattias's project yet, or Victoria's, but students aren't required to reveal their ideas ahead of time. The only requirement is to present in the Tank. Most classes wouldn't do well without a more concise set of checks and balances; but again, this isn't just any class. There is a lot of hushed conversation and top-secret stuff going on here. I occasionally spot check just to make sure everyone is making progress in the forward direction, answer questions, or brainstorm any supplies they might need. But really, if I vaporized into thin air, I'm not sure they would notice–at least not until the bell rang. I wish I could use this kind of insanely engaging project for all my classes.

I am not used to having time on my hands during the school day, but I think I've put it to good use: finding a competition pathway for Izzie.For the past two weeks, while my students have been busy solving Earth's environmental crisis project by project, I've been researching state and national science fair-type competitions for Izzie. There are surprisingly few options available for middle school students, particularly when you veer away from engineering into the so-called "soft sciences." Last year I sent a student to a national competition with her engineered therapy soccer ball... But, of course, that won't work for an environmental science project–even one as groundbreaking as Izzie's. A lot of middle school scientists compete at the national level via the Broadcom Masters, but it's a nomination-only competition that recruits candidates based on their results at the state science fair–so that one is out, too. Most of the application deadlines have passed.

But as it turns out, this environmental science class is connected to the high school Future Farmers of America (FFA) program. (I guess I should have realized this all along, but I've been a little busy the past few months developing a brand-new class–not just new to me, but to the entire state, so I am on my own.) FFA hosts its own unique fair system statewide. The high school FFA coordinator, Jenn, sent me an email yesterday with fair details and registration links. I have a week to help Izzie register and submit all her paperwork for competition, which is in April. Luckily, the paperwork is minimal–a few forms and a parent signature.

The hard part will be convincing her this is a valuable use of her time.

I wish Ira were here today, but he is on vacation and won't be back in class for two weeks. God-fucking-damn it; I wish he hadn't taken vacation right now. He is the Izzie whisperer. I am not.

I have made some inroads with Izzie over the past months. Building trust has been a slow process; our relationship is fragile, tenuous, delicate. I cannot push her into this opportunity. I can guide and encourage, but ultimately taking action is in her control, not mine. Since I know I can't sell her on this idea, I must find a more indirect route. Maybe in the end she'll sell herself on it.

Are my motives pure? Why is her participation so important to me? Is this about me and my ego, or about building her self-esteem and helping her find a place where she can experience real success? Maybe I need to soul search a bit before I call her up to my desk.

One of Izzie's superpowers is she is the ultimate bullshit meter. Life has taught her too many hard lessons. My brain concocts a quick outline of what I will say to her. With only a week to go, time is not on our side. This opportunity will not wait, so neither can I.

Two deep breaths. Breathe in, breathe out. And again.

Present your ideas; don't push. Be patient. Accept no.

Izzie looks up and we make eye contact across the room. She grins. It's time.

April: Days 132-149

Crunch Time

M iddle school has been a great experience. I had way more freedom, but it came with more responsibility.
It helped me grow a lot as a learner and a person.

Cooper D., 14

Day 136.5
8:51 a.m.

've been in the Grand Pavilion at the state fair once or twice, but until this morning, I didn't realize how large it was. The area is relatively quiet for a Saturday morning, but the crowds will make their way in as the day progresses. The section cordoned off for the FFA State Finals isn't obvious, so I wander for a few minutes through flower displays that already sport red and blue ribbons. The roses are particularly beautiful–I tend to a rose garden at home, so I can appreciate the care and love that nurtured these award winners. "Blue Girl" is a light lavender-colored rose with a strong spicy scent. My favorite. Apparently, the judges felt the same way: its vase is already adorned with a large, green "Best in Class" ribbon.

8:57 a.m.

Jenn is already at the booths. Our students' display boards, organized by division and category, were set up the night before by fair officials,. FFA students can compete in six primary categories including plant, environmental, and animal sciences. There are dozens and dozens of boards representing students from across the state.

I scan the area. No Izzie.

That's okay–she has a few minutes before our official call time. I hope she isn't late. I check my phone in case she texts me. Nothing.

I wait.

9:04 a.m.

I spot her as soon as she arrives, walking with an older girl who must be her sister. They have the same light brown hair, angular faces, straight noses. Watching them approach from a comfortable distance, I can sense their vibe; the attitude and energy is more than a family trait. It is forged from similar experiences.

Izzie spies me through the crowd as her sister turns to leave. She smiles and looks a little relieved.

"I wasn't sure we were in the right spot," she offers.

"Yes, this is exactly the right place." I pause. "You look nice, Izzie."

And she does. I can tell she took time to get ready this morning. She has applied a little bit of eye make-up–a careful compromise between her normal heavy-handed look and wearing none at all. Her hair is shiny and falls in waves across her shoulders–a perfect complement to the somewhat staid and professional look of the required FFA uniform: knee-length black skirt, white button-up collared blouse, and black flats. She doesn't own the signature blue jacket, but Jenn has a few extras and together we manage to find one that fits. It's hard to believe this is the same teenager who wears jeans that are theatrically ripped and shredded with belly shirts and crop tops that don't merely violate, but rather obliterate, our school dress code.

"Thanks, Mrs. C." Izzie looks away, almost shyly. "My sister helped me get ready. We had a hard time finding a skirt, though. We couldn't find anything that fit me."

She tugs at the hem, which is starting to slip down past her knees. Izzie is going to have a miserable time if she's worried about losing her skirt all day. She doesn't need one more distraction or complication. Today should be as obstacle-free as possible.

"Will you let me take a look? I might be able to fix it."

9:09 a.m.

One paper-clip fastener later, and her skirt isn't going anywhere. Apparently, necessity really is the mother of invention.

9: 45 a.m.

Round One begins in 15 minutes. Judges will preview projects one at a time; competitors stand quietly aside, seen but not heard. It is a nerve-wracking time for the competitors. Izzie and I have practiced this part during our after-school sessions. Silence is a learned skill.

The real competition takes place behind a curtained area during Round Two. Category specialists will scrutinize every detail of each project. Students will endure intense interviews. Some will emerge triumphant, and others defeated. Izzie has some real competition; there are several excellent projects in her division–thoughtful, well-researched, interesting, creative. I would not want to be a judge and am glad, for once, my place is on the sidelines. The remainder of the day is out of my hands. Izzie's success or failure rests squarely on her shoulders. She wouldn't want it any other way.

In FFA, only the first-place winners for each division and category can be considered for nationals. It is a brutal system that eliminates most competitors. All state winners must submit their lengthy, tedious applications by mid-June. By August, state winners are ranked, and only the top 12 are invited to attend and compete at nationals. There are no guarantees.

10:45 a.m.

Teachers and coaches are not allowed in the competition arena during the judging sessions, so I wait outside until Round One is finished. There will be a short break between sessions. A few more minutes.

This seems like a good time to text Ira. He is stuck in Maine this weekend, attending a family reunion. It's been planned for months. I know he is waiting for my updates.

"We're in Round One," I tell him.

"How's my starfish?"

"She's ready."

"Remind her it is all about the interview," he insists. "The judges want to know what she knows."

He's right. All the months of preparation really boil down to 10 minutes in front of the category experts. It doesn't matter how well-designed the board is, or how expertly data has been calculated and displayed. A well-written analysis from one contestant won't trump a spectacular interview from another. Knowledge combined with passion always wins.

"Give her a high-five and congratulations from me. Tell her I am proud of her for being there today."

"Of course."

There is an entire fair to explore, but I am stuck in place, sipping bad vendor coffee from a Styrofoam cup. Fairgoers stream past me, headed to the Home Living Expo Hall located next to the Pavilion. I amuse myself by pondering the irony of the young scientists in the building behind me offering inventions and ideas designed to advance technology, reduce pollution, and address global issues like climate change, while fair vendors are still allowed to dish their provisions into one of the most environmentally risky inventions in existence. I can't bring myself to throw away my empty cup, so I stuff it into my jacket for now. I wish I had brought a bigger purse.

10:56 a.m.

"Dr. Allen texted while you were in Round One. He said to tell you he is proud of you."

Izzie smiles. His words are important to her.

"How are you feeling?

She pauses. "I'm good." She's in her groove of quiet introspection.

She doesn't need any reassurances or overtures of luck.

I search for the most genuine emotion I can find. No sticky notes this time. I have about 90 seconds to let her know how much she deserves to be here. How proud I feel. How honored. How much I believe in her.

"Izzie, I am not going to wish you luck, because you don't need luck."

She looks me right in the eye–she is listening intently, ready to ferret out any placating remarks, but there are none. Perhaps I have been her teacher, but Izzie has taught me, too. She has taught me to be honest in all things. Straightforward. To give credit only when credit is due.

"Izzie," I continue. "You are an incredibly hard-working and talented young scientist. Your work is thoughtful and creative. I am proud you never gave up, no matter how difficult things became this year. You absolutely deserve to be here today. You don't need luck, because you have talent. Go in there and show those judges what you are made of. Go be amazing."

She doesn't say anything, but her eyes are smiling.

As I start to step away, she reaches towards me, and gives me a hug. It is an awkward little side hug–as if she can't quite decide whether it would be okay to hug me. Her arm gently sweeps my jacket, barely touching my back, and she steps into my side and crunches the Styrofoam cup. The sound startles her. Then we laugh.

It is the briefest gesture.

But it is a hug.

2: 23 p.m.

Jenn just got the word: the awards ceremony will begin at 3.

I text Izzie.

"Please be back at the Pavilion by 2:50 for the awards ceremony." I pad the time a little. I am not sure if Izzie is punctual or not. My only experience with her is from school, and we have bells there. I re-read my message and it seems a little stilted, so I add, "I hope you are having fun now that the judging is over!"

In her usual style, she sends a simple, "Okay."

2:45 p.m.

Izzie and another competitor are going to be re-interviewed. It is an unprecedented move by the judges- Jenn told me she's never heard of this in all her years of FFA competitions. Apparently, there is a tie. Izzie is tied for first place, and there cannot be a tie. Only one student will be advanced for consideration to attend nationals. There will be an additional judge this time, to break the tie.

I scan the entrance for her arrival. There is a tiny part of my brain that wonders if Izzie will indeed return to the Pavilion, but when I see her wavy brown hair bobbing towards me, I suddenly feel foolish. Even a little ashamed. How could I have doubted her?

"Where do we go for the awards ceremony, Mrs. C?

"The ceremony will be held right over there," and I point to the corner where volunteers are setting up a small podium and risers, presumably for pictures after. "It's going to be delayed a few minutes..." I begin. Izzie looks annoyed. Super annoyed.

"Mrs. C, you could have texted me. I was next in line for the Zipper. I waited in that stupid line for, like, 20 or 30 minutes. Now I gotta get in line all over again." Her face is pouting.

Ah yes. There is the surly teenager I know. And love.

I take a breath. "Izzie, I didn't text you because the judges want to re-interview you. Well, you and one other student. You are in a tie for first place."

Annoyance has been replaced by shock, and then excitement. Months and months of careful work and planning coalesce into this one tiny moment. Out of the corner of my eye, I see a judge signaling. They are ready for her. I ignore them to buy us a few more precious seconds.

"What should I talk about? I already did my whole presentation this morning. And answered a bunch of questions."

"Remember when we talked about 'next steps?'" Izzie nods. "I think the judges would be interested to hear about your future plans for this project—how you'd like to expand your original concept and 3-D print a filtration system that could be used to protect the barnacles."

"Should I just...tell them?"

"Well, wait until they ask you if there is anything else you'd like them to know about your project. That would be the perfect time."

"Okay Mrs. C. I've got this." Izzie turns towards the judges, who are motioning to her by the open curtain. She looks confident. Mature. She looks like a young woman who is ready to change the world.

Yes, you do, Izzie. Yes, you do.

3:14 p.m.

Division One winners are being announced first. The risers are populated with category winners from plant sciences, animals, and renewable energy. Two more, and then environmental science.

I scan the crowd, looking for Izzie's sister. I wonder if she made it here in time. Win or lose, it would be good for Izzie to have her family here. The area for guests and competitors is crowded—it is standing room only. Anxious parents in the back are sardining the people in front of them as they try to get a closer view.

A teenage boy in the standard blue FFA jacket cuts through the crowd and onto the risers. I can't hear his name, but there are cheers. Applause. One more to go.

3:15 p.m.

Isn't there a Tom Petty song about waiting? The waiting is the hardest part? *God, I miss Tom Petty.*

The room is hot, and I need to pee.

3:15:30 p.m.

There is a man deftly making his way through the crowd. I am distracted by his cunning, cat-like moves. He waits for a tiny opening and pounces, sliding his slender body into the open space. With every slide, he moves closer to me. He is young. Well, he is young-ish, but his face is old: tanned, with thick, heavy lines cutting through his cheeks and forehead. Weathered. His shoulders are slightly hunched. He looks tired. And determined.

As he turns in profile to face the podium, I see his angular jaw. Straight nose. I know that jaw. I recognize the nose.

3:17 p.m.

The crowd is too loud, and I am too far away from the podium to hear names. I see a head moving towards the podium—a head with wavy brown hair.

As Izzie steps onto the risers, my voice erupts in cheers. I can't whistle, so I clap and yell. Izzie's father is yelling, too. And clapping loudly.

We make eye contact. He is smiling. He is crying.
Me too.

3:18 p.m.
"Your starfish won!"
"Of course, she did," Ira replies. "How could she not?"

Day 140

"**S**o, what you are telling us, Mrs. C, is we have a choice?" Jay asks.

"Yes, yes you do. Whatever we decide as a class is what will happen, period." My voice is firm. Insistent.

And I am lying.

I am lying my ass off.

I don't normally make it a habit to lie to my students, but in this particular case, the lie is warranted.

I am 25 minutes into an intense discussion with my "honors" science class. It is not officially an honors class, but as a result of the master schedule that groups students by ability and funnels them into appropriate language arts and math classes–geometry versus 8th grade math, honors language arts versus regular or intervention classes, special education, etc.–I end up with one science class each year with a high proportion of students who are gifted or high achieving in math or language arts, or both. Of course, this doesn't necessarily mean they will be high achieving in science; it just means there is a certain sense of entitlement surrounding the idea of being in this class. They didn't earn the right to be here, but many of them don't understand the difference. And due to the master schedule, testing, and grouping of students, these same students end up in the same classes together all the way through middle school. By 8th grade, they become a bit of a clique: cool, but snobby. Exclusive. They joke and tease and fight, like siblings or cousins.

I love their sense of humor and the fact they get my ridiculous jokes. I love being able to talk with them about string theory and Newtonian versus Einsteinian physics. They delight in correcting my misspellings or pointing out my love of dangling participles. They are amusing and fun. Brilliant.

By the time they finish their freshmen year of high school, this clique will disband. But for now, they are firmly entrenched in believing they have somehow earned a spot in this glorious paradise of a class.

And their world is about to come crashing down.

For the first time since the bell rang, the class is quiet. Contemplative.

Clarissa breaks the silence.

"He's just a mean kid, you know." There are nods of agreement from around the room. "I see him every morning storming through the halls, running into people and shoving them into lockers. He laughs about it, too."

"Do you really think he is mean, or just out of control?" I counter. I know his meds don't kick in until the middle of first period, even on the best days. I can't talk to the class about Micah's ADHD or his floundering attempts with medication. That is confidential information. If they figure it out on their own, fine. But I can't add to the conversation.

Jay chimes in, "I don't think he is trying to be mean, but he ends up hurting people all the time."

"Yeah–he ran into me and left a bruise on my arm. My parents were so mad!" Zoe exclaims.

The room is now animated with the sharing of stories and remembrances from all corners of the room. Injustices, hurt feelings, bystander trauma–it all comes out, raw and unfiltered, polluting the psychology of the room. I notice Natalie, quiet amid the chaos. She is listening, observing.

"Why should we allow him into our class?" Zoe adds. "Isn't he in one of your afternoon classes? Shouldn't he just stay there? I don't think it is a good idea to put him here. Most of us have had some experiences with Micah that were... unpleasant." She pauses, gathering her words carefully. "I am not saying he is a bad person or anything. I am just saying I think he will have a rough time going to a new class away from his friends."

I cringe at the use of the word allow. Maybe I've let this go too far, but I don't see any other way around it. The class needs to believe they have a say in the decision to move Micah to honors science. If they think for a moment the decision was made without them, that his presence is being forced upon them, they will ostracize him for the remaining 40 days of school. Unfortunately, this decision was made without them–and without me. So, I must become the ultimate salesperson. I must persuade them to embrace an unsavory new reality. And I must trust my relationship with the class is strong enough to survive this hiccup.

I don't have the luxury of deciding whether moving him is a good decision. Micah has a debilitating conflict with another student in 5th period. There is no place else to move him except this class, without disrupting his entire schedule. Micah desperately needs this change of pace and a fresh start. But it won't work unless, somehow, I can get the class to agree en masse they are part of the solution. I sense we are reaching some type of ethereal tipping point—a place from which there is no return...

...We are tipping in the wrong direction.

It isn't my place to try to sway them or command a decision. Compliance is not the same thing as acceptance. I decide to gently counter Zoe's viewpoint.

"I think this class has a lot to offer someone like Micah. You have gifts and talents—talents others will never have. Maybe you should consider reaching out to him, even though he probably doesn't deserve you. Perhaps he does not deserve your kindness. That doesn't mean you shouldn't offer."

The class is dead silent. I swear I can even hear the digital clock humming overhead, ticking off the seconds. Maybe what I hear is the thumping of my heart, instead—my blood pumping anxiously as I wait for this jury to reach its final verdict.

I wait and watch. There is no general look of approval. No smiles or nodding heads. Their collective silence screams at me, "You are wrong, Mrs. C! He doesn't deserve us, or our kindness. And he especially doesn't deserve your love."

Their silence is overpowering, until the sudden scraping of a chair across the tile floor breaks the impasse. I turn to see Natalie standing up. She pushes her chair all the way back, ensuring she has everyone's attention. She keeps one hand on her chair to steady an almost-imperceptible quiver.

Her voice is clear and confident. "I agree with Mrs. C. I think we have an obligation to share our talents and gifts with others. I know many of us have had bad experiences with Micah, but maybe we can help him. Maybe by being in this class, we can help him make better choices. It won't be easy for us, but I imagine it will be worse for him to leave the people he feels comfortable around."

She turns to face me.

"Mrs. C., you can put him in a group next to me. I'll take care of him."

Clarissa chimes in. "Me too. I'll sit with him too."

Then Zoe. And Jay.

And in an instant, the wall comes tumbling down.

May: Days 150-170

Agony

've been a student for almost a decade now, and for many of those years it's been required that I do state testing. When I was younger, I didn't think too hard about why I had to do them, but I never liked them. Now that I've been doing them for so long, I realize how pointless and unnecessary state testing really is. For almost an entire month, students like myself are trapped in classrooms for hours on end, required to complete testing that has no real purpose. There are so many other possibilities of assignments or anything else that would be a much better use of time than a state-required test with scores we won't even find out until months later.

There is no way to describe state testing...other than it is irritating and pointless.

Natalie S., 13

Day 150.5

There are two reasons I would seriously consider leaving the classroom, the first being the never-ending barrage of meetings, trainings, and events only narrowly related to my day-to-day teaching responsibilities. I've imagined—fantasized, actually—a multitude of scenarios where I stand up in the middle of a staff meeting or inane training, grab my bag, and just leave. I'd walk calmly and unapologetically to my car and drive away. It would be a permanent extrication from the administrative bullshit that has very little to do with the work of teaching our kids, and everything to do with creating a façade of accountability to the public. The other reason is on my desk, beckoning to me from a pile of announcements, science publications, catalogs, and neatly paperclipped flyers I was supposed to hand out to my 6th period students, but which have now lost their relevance. Oh, well. I grab the flyers and chuck them into the recycle bin, paper clips and all. I add the catalogs and publications to a large stack behind my desk. As I finish my coffee, I congratulate myself on this marginal attempt at organization.

I can no longer delay or avoid.

It's time.

It's time, damn it.

For the past few days I've been reshuffling the carnage on my desk into neat little stacks in an attempt to avoid the unavoidable: the state testing manual that underscores the upcoming marathon of student testing. Its title assaults me in boldface Times New Roman: Smarter Balanced Assessment Consortium. Its presence bellows like a foghorn cutting through the quiet and calm of my Sunday morning classroom. May is the unofficial start of testing season—a period which will systematically derail classroom learning and instead focus on taking a summative snapshot of learning based on a randomly selected set of questions that, without question, are designed for a white, middle class demographic. While all students should have been introduced to the relevant content, the context of the questions alienate nontraditional learners, minorities, students with learning disabilities, and students in poverty. State testing is designed to separate the achievers and nonachievers—as crudely and callously as separating wheat from chaff. It is not a celebration of learning. In our public attempt to maintain standards and hold schools and teachers accountable for student learning of basic skills, we have created a system that rewards excellence in academic testing, not learning. While some universities, including the ivy leagues, have abandoned the requirement for precollege exams, recognizing their inherent unfairness as well as their irrelevance in predicting future success, state-mandated school systems still cower to the demand for public accountability. In this system, the Izzies and Micahs of the world don't stand a chance.

My Izzies. My Micahs.

I take their accomplishments personally.

Micah's transfer to honors science has been extraordinarily successful–better than I had hoped, considering the rough start. His charm has worked its magic on most of the class. He routinely sneaks bags of Cheetos into class in his backpack and offers handfuls to anyone who will sit with him during work time. I like to tease him about his Cheetos–my favorite snack food–and I started requiring he pay a "Cheetos tax" on every bootleg bag. It is our little joke. I pretend not to see his Cheetos transgressions, and he pays up with a napkin full of snackage left neatly on my desk. A little extortion is a good life lesson.

He has quickly wormed his way into Natalie's group, as if he belonged there all along. She calls them the 'Fantastic 5.' The group mentor him through the curriculum he has missed, but they won't let him copy, and they call him out on any ridiculous behavior. His meds are helping. He still isn't on the right dose, or the best brand, but even these half-measures have had an impact. His grade has climbed from an F to a solid, consistent C-. His transformation over the past six weeks has been nothing short of miraculous. But it won't be enough; not for the state, not for the public blinded by the ruse of accountability. Micah will never pass a state exam. I can only hope that the progress he is making right now, and his social skills, will sustain him and help him realize that he has a place where he can fit it, a path by which to forge his own success.

And Izzie? We've spent countless hours since April working together after school on her application for Nationals. It still blows my mind to imagine that she could be in the top 12–we won't know until later this summer. While our relationship has warmed considerably, I cannot take the credit for her success. By opening her door to Ira, she created a path to find her own success. She reached out to an adult that she could connect with–one that she could trust. She has gained real confidence in her own abilities. But, despite her accomplishments in FFA, her many absences have affected her learning. I am not sure that her emerging self-confidence can handle a dose of state-mandated failure.

I can't help but worry.

In a perfect world, I would abolish state testing completely—an idea long overdue and embraced by those countries now leading the way forward in education reform. I'd focus my time and energy on creating a continuous learning environment, so rich and supportive that every student would be able to create their own version of success.

Huh. Wouldn't that be something?

For now, I have no choice but to lead my students forward into the dark abyss of public accountability and hope that the connections we've built and successes they have experienced will be enough to sustain them when the system fails them.

I hope it is enough.

It has to be.

Day 168

And just like that, she is gone.
I didn't see it coming.
I should have, shouldn't I?
But I didn't.

The light pouring into my classroom from the windows that line the far wall casts eerie shadows between each desk from the chairs still stacked on top.

The clear intensity of this sunrise promises a gorgeous day ahead.

But I am stuck in those shadows; their predictable pattern is calming. My eyes flit back and forth, row after row, taking some solace in their familiarity. The pattern stops. There is a single spot, standing out like the brilliance of a yellow highlighter marking up a faded grey document.

Just a desk without a chair. Her desk. No shadow, –just light. How completely ironic to witness light, rather than darkness.

No one bothered to put her chair up. It remained untouched–out of reverence, or fear, or maybe apathy–or maybe just a lapse in memory. I first heard about her near the end of the day yesterday. Overlooked amid bells, and the loudspeaker announcement about the cancelled baseball practice, and the end of the day commotion, many of my students had not.

They will know today.

As I watch the shadows and now the light, I revel in the early morning quiet– a sharp contrast to the cacophony of questions and subsequent blame attacking my subconscious. Our morning custodian, Gino, has arrived and I hear him opening hallway doors. The rumbling boilers interrupt me only long enough to let me catch my breath before the rapid-fire assault of my thoughts begins again.

School won't start for another two hours. I need the time to manifest a sense of normalcy for today. As I open my email, I see there is a message to all staff. "Grief counselors will be available for students and staff all day. Please send any students who are struggling or need emotional assistance to the main office. It will be beneficial to maintain a sense of normalcy and routine for your classes today as we deal with this terrible loss."

A loud snort punctuates the silence, followed by loud, gasping laughs, and I realize those are my snorts and my laughs. I make a conscience effort to control the noises erupting from my mouth and nose to reread, "available to students and staff all day..." and marvel at the ridiculousness of this inane promise. There is no time for staff to receive counseling at school. Not today or any other day. Yes, they are required to offer us assistance, if we can make our way to the main office, wait our turns to cry and mourn and spill out our guts for 10 or 12 minutes as we watch the digital displays overhead that remind us our planning periods are over, and listen for the final bell that calls us back to class. There simply isn't time. There is never time. Not to pee or eat a proper meal, let alone say, "I am distraught and need help. Please cover my class so I can work through my pain." I know my pain won't bring me to the brink of suicide. My needs are less; my priority must be my students. I have read the statistics and heard the stories: One student's suicide can precipitate more student suicides. I do understand that the guidance counselors are there to help the students. Offering help to staff is required; the real-world application of this offer is just that—an offer. This knowledge doesn't make me feel better. I feel resentful that my needs are less. I feel a twinge of guilt for even having needs. But I am the adult here, and my needs always come second. I know this. I am done laughing now and I am left with frustration. And sadness. And shadows.

I still have 1 hour and 43 minutes to work through my pain and loss and self-blame, and I will have to do it alone, in the shadows, so I can create that "routine and sense of normalcy" in my classroom. Except it will not be routine or normal today. Or tomorrow.

Will time erase her story completely, or just dull it enough to make her memory tolerable?

I should find her things while my room is quiet and dark and shadowy. Will her parents want those assorted remnants of their daughter? I don't know. It just seems like the right thing to do—to gather her papers and reports and science journal and deliver them to someone with more authority than me, someone who can decide which remnants to keep and which to throw away. At least, those are my intentions. I have several stacks of graded and ungraded papers to rifle through, and as I pull her assignments and tests, I begin to fill a large manila envelope. I unlock a file cabinet next to my desk and pull out her file, where I've squirreled away several excellent examples of her work. They won't be used now for her end-of-year reflection, so those, too, I place in the envelope. At the bottom of the file I find the purple-flowered note she left me under my door months ago—another world ago. That is mine. I am sure her parents would appreciate seeing it, but I cannot part with it. Selfishly, I fold the note smaller and shove the bit of paper into my purse. I will find it later and maybe then I can give it the time and care it deserves.

There is only one more place I might find pieces of her that belong in the envelope. In the back of my classroom near the door are the bins of composition notebooks. I require my students to keep handwritten notebooks all year long. By now, these notebooks are chock full of lab write-ups and data tables, detailed Cornell notes, formulas for speed and velocity, Newton's laws—the list goes on and on. It takes me a moment to find her journal. No name on the front, but little pink flowers this time, instead of purple.

"Steps of the Scientific Method" is neatly taped on the inside of the front cover. On the next page is her copy of the metric ladder, clean and pristine and perfect. I don't mean to keep turning the pages, but each one represents a moment or an event. I can't help but smile picturing her during our first engineering challenge, her petite frame hidden completely behind the tower she created with tape and all kinds of straws organized to cantilever off the end of the lab table. I try to remember. Did her tower fall? She didn't win the challenge—I would have remembered such an important detail. Her success or failure is already a blur, like so many small details about her I overlooked. She didn't require my attention; she didn't need me for guidance or motivation. She was easy and undemanding. At least, that was what she wanted me to see.

Until now.

My finger happens upon a dog-eared page covered with doodles and shapes. Words.

I hate me. I hate me. I hate me. I love him. I hate me. I love him. HATE ME. ME ME ME

Him? Who is "him?" A secret crush? I rarely saw her with anyone—except the time she was working next to Brian during pizza night. He was always kind to her.

Her words assault my brain. I flip to the next page. And the next.

More words. Hateful. Self-deprecating. Now I can't unsee them, like one of those psychology tests I took in college for extra cash. I thumb through the rest of her journal, finding more secrets in margins: her pained musing hidden between Cornell notes and unit vocabulary. Taken out of context, out of the realm of current events, her words might be nothing more than normal teenage angst. Today's reality gives her words new weight.

I start tearing. The dog-eared page comes out, along with dozens of others. I rip carefully, acting as final editor; both judge and jury. Her parents have the right to her journal, but not the blame. I saw her journal every single week and never once stopped to read her interjections. If I had taken a moment to read her words, would I have recognized them as more than sulky scribblings? The pile of torn pages and jagged remnants is now too large to stuff into my purse with her note, so I eviscerate them until there are only tiny scraps left. I drop them slowly, methodically, into the recycle bin next to my desk. The Marie Kondo method of journal editing, I suppose. "Keep only what brings you joy."

I don't know if I have the right to or not, but it is done.

I slide the journal into the manila envelope. On the front I write, "To the Parents of KN."

I stack her chair. What remains of her is the pile of tiny secret words under my desk, muted for eternity.

23 minutes left to mourn.

Goodbye, sweet Kayla.

Day 170

To: All Staff
    Subject: FYI–Confidential

Dear Staff,

Late last night we received word that one of our students, Jetmir, was involved in a serious car accident. He is currently in critical condition at Children's Hospital. We will update you as soon as we receive more information.

Our counselor, Brian, will be the point of contact and will liaise with the family to offer any support they may need.

We will be organizing a collection to help the family with some of their immediate needs. There will be information in the staff lounge later today about how you may contribute to this fund.

Please keep information about Jetmir's condition confidential, as he has brothers and sisters in the district. Please refer any students who may need counseling or support to Brian.

My office door is always open.

Jim

Jim's door is always open. It's one of his most endearing qualities.

I am not sure how I will survive these final 10 days of school. Maybe now would be a good time to get in my car and never return. The unapologetic exit of my fantasies. This marks a third reason to leave, and by far the most compelling.

This would be the time. Except I cannot.

I must stay here and bear witness to their voices.
Their purpose.
Their message.

They must remain unmuted, in perpetuity.

Michele M. Chamberlain

June: Days 171-180

The Importance of Goodbyes

S chool is a place of growth more than it is a place of learning. All teachers should be familiar with the constantly repeated statistic about how much information students lose over summer break, and how much time is spent merely reteaching. But, while learning is important, school has never just been about curriculums or units. School is a place to grow. As time goes on, the memories students have of their schooling and their experiences with their teachers continues to fade, with only the most vivid memories staying with them. But school isn't about the memories. It's about growing. The children who wandered into your classroom in September have all gained something over the course of the year: a constant figure and place to go to. Like the way a bean plant's growth is dependent on their beanpole, by being there for your student every day this year, you have let them grow into something more. This doesn't mean that every student will admit it, however; even I can look back at myself two years ago and still feel like the same person I was, despite being in high school now. But I have different experiences now. I've met more people, I've had different interests to pursue, and I've had different constants to return to; the last being the reason why the school year must end. Summer is a time to embrace that last aspect of our growth and do something with it. So, even if we forget your face, your name, your voice, and anything you've ever taught us, just know that we still have changed because of you, and that we can tell that you have as well. For that reason, make the goodbyes count, so we can all continue to grow.

Mattias S., 16

Day 174

I t's a beautiful June afternoon. For now.

Weather in the Pacific Northwest during this time of year is famously unpredictable. While winters are grey and overcast and sport a continual layer of drizzle, late spring can vary from drenching rains to 80+ degree heat. My weather app is predicting a pleasant 74 degrees with a 30% chance of rain. In a different region of the country, this prediction could be sanely disregarded. But here, that would be a major mistake. I have decided to change into sensible shoes that will survive a sudden cloudburst. I've lived here too long to worry about an umbrella.

It was no surprise to any Northwest natives that Stephanie Meyer chose Forks as the setting for her wildly famous series about the vampire/wolf/Bella love triangle. Forks, of course, would be the area where vampires would choose to live. The area is infamous for its lack of sun and a dreariness that perpetuates year-round. As I walk towards St. John's Cathedral in my sensible shoes, I laugh a bit at the memory of a conversation about the "Edward versus Jacob" debate:

"Mrs. C," my 8th grade girls would ask me in hushed voices, "who do you think is hotter–Jacob or Edward?"

"Girls–really, I can't answer that question." I would always try to divert. "Who do YOU think is hotter?"

"Come on–please tell us," they would beg. "You've seen the movies, right?"

I would have to admit I saw the movies. And read the books. Teaching middle school means keeping up on teen culture. It does not, however, mean I am required to be part of Team Jacob or Team Edward.

I would usually be able to put this conversation to rest by pointing out to them the grossness of their suggestions. "Look, ladies–Edward is 17. Yes, I know he is actually a 100-year-old vampire, but he is in a 17-year-old body. I am...well, I am over 40. So, don't you think it would be just a little bit pervy if I could tell you which one was hotter?" This would slow their insistent hounding.

"Really girls? You want hot? Okay–how about Sam Elliott? A young Robert Redford?"

They have no idea about the Sams and Roberts of the world, and at this point, the conversation stops completely. They don't want to hear about my ancient crushes.

The walk to the church is a few short blocks from school. Kayla's family arranged the funeral for today so that as many students as possible could attend. It was a classy move—to allow us to share this day so completely. School is still in session for the afternoon, but most students left with a parent right after lunch. Our administration and counselors stayed behind to cover our classes. I doubt there will be much for them to do.

I am brought back to the moment by the sight of police barricades redirecting traffic away from small streets immediately surrounding the entrance, while hundreds of well-wishers and mourners crowd the sidewalks. They spill out of the open cathedral doors and down its stairs, onto the manicured grass and hot pavement. The service won't begin for another 45 minutes and I am suddenly relieved I won't be able to go anywhere near those open doors. From my vantage point a block or two away, I hear crying and stifled sobs. I am gripped with anxiety that my calm demeanor—my lack of tears—will seem distant or disrespectful. My tears were spent privately; there are none left for public display. The grief that held me hostage for days has lessened its grip and changed into something entirely different and unexpected.

Grief to gratefulness.

I feel grateful.

Jim sent out an update this morning: Jetmir is stable. The accident caused a traumatic brain injury, and there was considerable swelling. Part of his skull was removed to allow room for his brain. He has a very long road ahead of him, and his odds of complete recovery are slim. But I know Jetmir. He is strong. Positive. Resilient. I am certain that he will be the one to beat those odds. "If it is Allah's will," he would tell me, with a radiant smile. "Allah's will in all things."

His family is keeping a round-the-clock vigil at the hospital. Our staff took up a collection for them earlier last week to help with some of the expenses, and we set up a rotating schedule for meals. We've been asked to drop off meals at school in the morning. Jim delivers them to the family in the evening. My day is tomorrow. I picked up a leg of lamb last weekend from Costco and it's waiting in my fridge to be roasted. I know how to prepare it according to Jewish customs, but his family is Muslim, so I am out of my depth. I don't think this lamb was slaughtered halal. The packaging says it was imported from Australia and there aren't a lot of Muslims in Australia; my quick internet search told me that number is about 2.6%, give or take. I trust that a benevolent Allah will overlook my ignorance this once and in accordance with the Quran, accept this meal to nourish their bodies.

I feel thankful.

There is such an outpouring of support from her classmates today. Kayla wasn't a popular student. She wasn't involved in sports or cheer or other extracurriculars. She didn't have many close friends. She was quiet and solitary and, as it turned out, suffering from a pain that none of us could see. There were no alarm bells to warn us of her impending doom; or maybe there were, but we missed them. She managed to slip through our lives undetected until, for her, life was no longer a viable option. Her death has etched a memory on our hearts in a way her life did not.

I feel determined.

Kayla's is not the first student funeral I've attended, but it will be the last. It must be. Can I advocate for my students in all things; unrelenting? Am I strong enough to hear their stories? Can I find them the help they need? I don't know.

Here is what I do know: there will be no more slipping through the cracks. I must get better at seeing them, at recognizing their quiet, almost-imperceptible cries for help. Breaking their barriers. It is literally a matter of life or death.

A makeshift memorial has been growing directly in my path. It stretches half the length of a city block and ends a few feet from where I am standing. A large purple heart is attached to the fence above a trove of stuffed animals, cards, and flowers.

The rain that has been threatening all day now speckles the sidewalk and street, but there is no danger of a real soaking. The rain feels fresh and clean on my face and bare arms. The air has turned slightly muggy—too warm for a jacket. I wish now I had worn my sandals. My feet feel hot and sticky inside their closed toes. As I bend over to unfasten my shoes and peel off my socks, I notice a little purple rabbit in the line of stuffies, outfitted in a yellow rain slicker. I can't help but laugh: Apparently, someone else paid attention to the weather report. He looks snug, tucked between flowers and cards. A bouquet of daisies sticks up over his hood and it looks like he is under a tiny canopy of white petals.

I haven't brought anything to add to the memorial. I intended to, but the roses I carefully cut from my garden in the predawn morning were abandoned in my haste to change into sensible shoes and double-check the weather. Too late now—by the time I return to my classroom, they will be wilted beyond hope. My good intentions have left me empty-handed.

I am saved by the unintentional.

It takes me a minute, but I rummage in my purse for her note. The one with tiny purple flowers that she left under my door so many months ago. I smooth the crumpled edges, then fold it into a tiny, precise square, just the right size to tuck into the pocket of a certain yellow rain slicker.

It seems like the right thing to do.

Day 179

"**M**rs. C, I would like to thank you so much for being my teacher. Before I came to this class I disliked science and wanted nothing to do with it. Now, after being in your class, I want to take a career in astrophysics. Words cannot describe how grateful and honored I am to be your student."
Jay

"Mrs. C- thank you for being an outstanding teacher. Your snacks and puzzles are AWESOME. You made science FUN! "
Kiara

"You've taught me so much, and I am very thankful I was put in your class. You have pushed me to love science even more."
Aden

For my 8th graders, there are certain rites of passage that occur these final two days of school: cleaning out lockers and desks, returning overdue library books and team uniforms, paying fines, turning in those last-minute, last-second, grade-altering assignments, assemblies and awards, and talent shows. The commotion which marks the passing of our final precious hours together underscores the finality of their middle school years. For some, there is relief and excitement for the future. For others, sadness in the realization that this—arguably the final vestige of their childhood—is at its conclusion.

There is no event more instrumental in celebrating this rite than the signing of yearbooks.

I am ready. I have my collection of pens: roller balls that won't bleed through the pages. When the first bell rings, Heather and I will connect our rooms so students can wander back and forth. By this afternoon, the entire 8th grade hallway will be open, and students will sit in corners and find quiet classrooms, writing their goodbyes and memorializing friendships.

As they wander, many will find their way to my room.

The bell won't announce first period for another 25 minutes, but my door opens, and I hear Jay's voice.

"Mrs. Chamberlain?" he hesitates. "Can I come in?"

"Of course, Jay! You're here early. Is everything okay?" I stand up and walk towards him as he enters the class.

He is suddenly shy and 8th-grade-boy inarticulate. "Yes, uhm. I'm fine." He can't quite get the words out. I know why he is here.

"Hey, Jay, I picked up my yearbook this morning. I would be honored if you would sign it for me"

"Yeah, I just got mine too. Can you sign mine?"

"I would love to, Jay. Thank you so much for asking me."

And so, we sit in silence, pausing to find just the right words to say how we feel, to encapsulate an entire year together in just two or three lines.

"You are by far the coolest teacher I've ever had–from letting us give haircuts to playing cards! I'm so lucky to have had you. The Fantastic 5 will miss you forever."
Natalie

"Thank you for always snacking us, even in 6th period, and making this class fun. I am really gonna miss you."
Mason

"I love you soooo much. I am so happy I had you as a teacher."
Mariah

To sweeten some of the bittersweet of this day, I tell my students that when I am an old lady, I will pack this collection of yearbooks with me to the old folks' home to freshen my recollections. I tell them I will remember them fondly, that I won't forget them, that I will brag about their accomplishments to all of my little old lady friends and say, "I remember them! Those were my students!"

Sometimes their entries are silly, with things like "H.A.G.S" or "I will come visit you." Silly because, with rare exceptions, most of them won't come visit. At least, not yet. And that is how it should be. This is a time to look forward, not cling to the past.

"You've taught me more than science. You've taught me how to be more open-minded, and to have patience, and love everyone. PS: I love your red hair."
Clarissa

"Much love, many wows."
Micah

But I won't wait until I am old to open these books. I look at these books every year. They inspire me at the start of each new school year.

As I rifle through the pages, I return instantly to our time together.

"I am glad this has been one of your favorite years of teaching, because it has been one of my favorite years of learning. We learn best when everyone is having a good time, which is every day in your class."
Mattias

"Thank you, thank you for the fun, amazing and educational year."
Sammie

"I learned so many things about how much we have messed up our world, and I have become more and more interested in learning how to fix it. You are truly talented at bringing out the best in people."
Camden

"Thank you for being such a blessing in my life. Oh—and I am sorry for the really bad handwriting."
Josh

"Remember me, your favorite student!"
Daljit

I know that at some point, our paths will cross again—some sooner, and some much later. But until they do, I reread their words and count myself fortunate to have known them.

They are my past, and our collective future.

They are the problem solvers. The peacekeepers. The leaders. The caretakers.

We are in good hands.

Michele M. Chamberlain

Epilogue

I n August of the same year, the national FFA rankings were released, and Izzie's name was among them. She traveled with the high school team later that fall to Minneapolis to compete with her Environmental Science project. She placed 5th at Nationals. Her incredibly stubborn nature and resilient attitude continue to keep her focused despite life's challenges and disappointments. Dr. Allen asks about Izzie every time I see him. He remains persistent in keeping his starfish safe in the ocean.

Jetmir spent his freshman year of high school in and out of the hospital. It's been seven years since his accident. His recovery has been slow, but steady; his spirit remains undeterred. With the support of his family and friends, he earned his high school diploma. He would still like to become a doctor and is starting online college in the fall.

Micah still struggles with the effects of his ADHD but is learning to navigate life and school. The friendships he built in 4th period science continue today. Every time I eat Cheetos, I think of him and smile.

"Kayla" is a fictional character who represents two male students of mine who died by suicide. I've woven their stories together to bring a lens to the problem of teen suicide. While girls attempt suicide at higher rates, boys die by suicide four times as often. Just like the character Kayla, my students who died were both quiet boys who kept to themselves. As they slipped in and out of my class, day after day, it never crossed my mind that they might be at risk, until it was too late.

10% of the profits from the sale of this book are being donated to the American Foundation for Suicide Prevention.

Afterward

The mental health concerns affecting children in this book and ranging from ADHD to trauma from bullying to self-harm may come as a surprise to no reader. It's not a secret that children in the United States face more mental health issues–and more severe ones, at that–than perhaps ever before. If the statistics were surprising or the consequences worrisome, it is time to act.

Chances are, every reader knows a child who is struggling with various mental health difficulties that may or may not lead to suicidal ideation, or the desire to kill oneself. Many readers have even dealt with these issues themselves. Whether you're personally familiar with the toll of mental illness or not, you are in a position to help those around you. We can each start by promoting mental health education and learning the warning signs that could point to a child in danger.

Potential warning signs of suicidal ideation:
- Withdrawing from family, friends, or peer interaction
- Researching methods of self-harm or suicide
- Quitting extracurriculars, hobbies, or other activities
- Becoming aggressive or irritable
- Displaying symptoms of depression such as hopelessness, perpetual fatigue, or isolation

Factors which may increase likelihood of suicide, suicide attempt, or suicidal ideation:

- History of abuse or family violence
- Substance use/abuse
- Experiencing bullying
- Physical health issues, chronic pain, or brain injury
- Extreme or traumatic life transitions, including parental divorce, moving, or financial stress
- History of suicide or suicide attempts in the family

While psychologists and mental health professionals have devoted countless hours to identifying certain risk factors, suicide and suicidal ideation can be unpredictable. Still, we owe it to children (and loved ones of any age) to be as vigilant as possible in seeing their struggles and providing assistance and resources.

If you are experiencing suicidal ideation or you believe someone you love may have suicidal thoughts or intent, here are some ways to seek help.

First and foremost, if you or someone you love is in immediate danger of harm, please dial 911 or your local emergency number immediately. You can also visit your nearest emergency room.

To speak with someone about suicidal thoughts, you can call the National Suicide Prevention Lifeline at 1-800-273-8255. This is a 24-hour helpline that provides free, confidential emotional support to anyone who calls. There is also an online chat function at https://suicidepreventionlifeline.org.

GoodTherapy is a website that provides news, articles, and other information about suicide and mental health. They also maintain an international directory of mental health professionals, so you can search for a therapist worldwide. Their mission to destigmatize mental health and promote nonpathologizing (person-first) psychotherapy sets GoodTherapy apart from other similar directories. Visit https://www.goodtherapy.org/ to learn more.

Psychology Today, a popular magazine and online resource, also hosts thousands of articles on various mental health topics, as well as a directory of psychotherapists. Search online at https://www.psychologytoday.com/us.

Local resources can also provide valuable assistance. Check to see if your area has a chapter of the American Foundation for Suicide Prevention (AFSP) or a family support center. Your child's school may have more information about local organizations that are tailored to your geographic location.

Note that these organizations are almost always looking for more volunteers to help disseminate information about suicide and the complications of mental health issues. Consider donating or getting involved on a local level. Doing so can help normalize mental health treatment and the act of communicating candidly about these serious issues that affect families every day.

The more we talk about suicide and mental health concerns, the more we can do to prevent fatal consequences. For anyone struggling: There is hope. Your story must continue.

Jo Sahlin

Made in the USA
Coppell, TX
30 April 2020